DON'T
DO STUFF
YOU
Suck AT

Roadmap to your Front Seat Life™ for entrepreneurs, direct sellers and others that want to change the world

Jessica Butts, MA

Copyright © 2017 Jessica Butts

Don't Do Stuff You Suck At: Roadmap to Your Front Seat Life for Entrepreneurs, Direct Sellers, and Others that Want to Change the World

All rights reserved. No part of this book may be reproduced, stored in a retrieval system or transmitted by any other means without the written permission of the publisher and author.

Jessica Butts
www.jessicabutts.com
ISBN: 978-0-9992884-0-5 (print book)
ISBN: 978-0-9992884-1-2 (eBook)

Cover design by Melina Creative

Interior text design and printing by Gorham Printing

Printed in the United States of America

Legacy ONE AUTHORS

Kirkland, WA
www.legacyoneauthors.com

DEDICATION

To my sister, Erica (and those like her who think they can't leave a job that sucks the life out of them). Not only can you do it, but you did it. You worked two jobs in the process and found a way because your passion for your life and what you want to do in this world is worth it. You didn't settle for fine; you choose to live extraordinary. I am so proud of you!

ACKNOWLEDGEMENTS

It takes a whole lot of work to run a business and write a book at the same time so I have some people to thank for helping me.

To my amazing clients for giving me as much as I give you. You continue to inspire me and build me up to keep pushing. Let's keep going. What do you say?

To my Front Seat Life Team of Experts, not only do you provide great service to my clients, but you give so much to me as well. Lisa Fischer, you are not only a friend and my stylist but truly one of the best people I have ever met. Pia Larson, thank you for your continued support as a friend and my web designer. You keep pushing me to become the person you see me as, which means the world to me. Jeni Dahn, my "being" coach, thank you for being the P to my crazy J. Nikki Rausch, thank you for teaching me how to invite people to be a part of the Front Seat Life way of life so they can change their lives. Debbie Rosemont, not only are you part of the team but also my mastermind group. Your beautiful S keeps me grounded…all the while still pushing me; it's a perfect combination. Nikki Closer, thank you for photographing me and my clients to bring out the authenticity in us. To Sarah Frink, thank you for being vulnerable enough when I met you to admit you needed help. Look how far you have come to living your life authentically and OUT LOUD. I love having you in my life. And lastly, Karen Lynn Maher, my friend and book coach, there is NO way *Live Your Life from the Front Seat* or this book could have been written without your experienced coaching. Thank you!

My accountability partner, Denise Lloyd, thank you for the years of phone calls and never letting me settle and helping me see clearly when I am stuck in the weeds.

Stephanie Wagner, my amazing assistant, thank you for doing all the stuff I suck at with a smile on your face!

To my mom, pop, and sister. Thank you for loving me for who I am, faults and all!

CONTENTS

Letter to My Readers ix

Introduction xv

SECTION 1

Roadmap to Who Are You?
Myers-Briggs Personality Type 1

    Nature vs. Nurture 3

    Introversion and Extroversion 15

    Sensing and Intuition 26

    Thinking and Feeling 38

    Judging and Perceiving 45

    Marginalized Types 57

    Whole Letter Type 59

    Group/Team Type 63

    Archetypical View 66

SECTION 2

Roadmap to Your Front Seat Life
Live Your Life from the Front Seat™ 73

    Live Your Life from the Front Seat 75

    Your Front Seat 82

Your Back Seat	87
Introverts: Your Car	95
Extroverts: Your car	113
Summary of Front Seat Activities	130
The Trunk of Our Cars	138

SECTION 3

Roadmap to Where Are You Going?
Up-Leveling Your Mindset	149
Up-Leveling Your Mindset	151

SECTION 4

Roadmap to How Are You Going to Get There?
Taking Action! The Three S Method™	183
Taking Action	185
About the Author	234

LETTER TO MY READERS

When I wrote my first book, *Live Your Life from the Front Seat* (2014), I had no idea if anyone other than my family would read it. I was terrified to put it out into the world. The process of writing that book helped me figure out who I was in this world and what my point of view is, which I discovered were not easy tasks. I was challenged with many limiting beliefs and damaging thoughts: I am not smart enough to write a book; nobody is going to read it; do I really have enough interesting information to fill a whole book? Then there was the mother of all doubt: what if people would hate my book?

It took me two and a half years to write *Live Your Life from the Front Seat* and I wouldn't change any painstaking moment of the process. By writing the book I got crystal clear on a lot of aspects of my business life:

- I know what I'm good at in the world.
- I understand my strengths.
- I know where to spend my time and energy to optimize my business success.
- I am clear about my singular business focus.
- I accept that not everyone is going to like me.
- I have something unique and powerful to share with the world.
- I must always, 100% of the time, show up unapologetically as who I am.
- And I need to not do stuff I suck at.

Luckily, you don't have to write a book to learn the same lessons because I'm going to teach you in this book. *Live Your Life from the Front Seat* is a wonderful and more general book about getting the things you want in life by understanding your innate personality type. This book does the same; however, it is more focused on business techniques for entrepreneurs and business owners. I am calling this work *Front Seat Life for Businesses.* It is the foundation of all the work I do with individuals, entrepreneurs, and couples who are embracing and rocking their innate personality types.

Like many of you, the experiences of my life drew me to my work. I became a psychotherapist and then a business coach because of my personal life. Like the saying goes, "My mess is my message." Well, my mess took me down the path of change and clarity, and I want desperately for you to choose the same path. It's a journey that will heal you.

I was born into a good family. My parents were loving, kind, responsible, and hard working. They divorced when I was young and they both did an amazing job raising me and my sister with love and respect. My mess didn't start until later in life and it took two forms, both of which drew me to my work. My whole life I felt like a weirdo, and my marriage had serious issues from the beginning. Both came to a head at the same time when I was in my mid-30s.

I met my husband in college. He was big man on campus—handsome, charismatic, athletic. I fell hard and fast and spent 20 years with him. We had what appeared to be a perfect life: house, no kids, travel. Except it wasn't perfect. I was living a life I knew in my gut wasn't the life God designed me to live. I didn't know what that life was, but I knew what I had wasn't it. Do you know this feeling?

For many of us, our twenties are hard as we try to figure out life—especially who we are and what our career path will be.

Then most of us get married. I honestly believe no one should get married until they are at least 30. Maybe it should be regulated like getting a driver's license at 16 and being able to legally drink at 21. Wouldn't that change the way we are in our twenties? So much of that decade is spent trying to please others (parents, friends, spouse, professors, bosses) and make big decisions (college major, career). Add on trying to find our mate. It's absurd. Our focus ought to be figuring out ourselves.

As a society, we are too outwardly focused on how others see and define us, which is crazy. As you can imagine, during my twenties I focused on everything and everyone but me and I completely lost myself. Does this sound familiar?

In 2006, the Universe responded to my thoughts and provided me a huge wake-up call. Four years into my marriage my husband came home to tell me he didn't know if he loved me anymore and was going to move out. I was devastated, lost, and scared. More than anything, though, I was angry at myself for not seeing it coming and for allowing it to happen. I asked, "Was I blind or just choosing not to see what was happening in my own home?" While he was battling his own demons and I was blaming him for destroying our marriage, my real growth came as I started to see my part in the mess. I had totally lost myself, lost my voice, lost my purpose, and lost my passion for him, myself, and my life.

I spent the next few months sitting on my kitchen floor bawling uncontrollably each night after work. Some people have "bathroom floor moments." Mine were kitchen floor moments. At age 32, I was broken and lost. I sat in self-pity for a few months and spent the next few years in and out of couples therapy. I moved out, moved back in, then back out. We went on trips together and even bought a new house to try and fix our marriage. Finally, our last therapist said to me, "Jessica, do you really want to be in this relationship?"

I was pissed. Why would I sit there doing all that work if I didn't want to be in the relationship? However, that question stayed with me for a long time before I decided to take action.

While my marriage was struggling, the company I worked for as a human resources specialist was laying people off. I walked straight into my boss' office and volunteered to leave (without having a plan). I knew I needed to do something different. It was in that job—after a string of boring, unfulfilling HR jobs—I realized I was different. I hated the 9-5 schedule, the details, the meetings that meant nothing, pretending to help people, and pushing paper. I hated my work, but everyone else seemed happy. What was going on? Why was I the only one who seemed miserable in the corporate world?

I was jobless and on the brink of divorce when I got the answer I needed. I went to a local Myers-Briggs meeting the Saturday after I had been laid off. The room was full of coaches and therapists and I had never felt more insignificant and lost. Yet I also felt exhilarated because everyone in the room had one thing in common: they were doing what I wanted to be doing. The following Monday I drove to the school, without an appointment, and told the receptionist I wanted to talk to someone about enrolling in the Masters of Counseling program to become a psychotherapist. Without the approval of my husband (and many naysayers telling me I didn't need to go back to school and incur the debt) I committed to graduate school that very day.

What I value most about my graduate studies was that I discovered me. I found my voice, my soul, and my purpose. I realized I no longer fit with my husband or with corporate America. As it turns out, I *am* a weirdo, an Intuitive Type (which you're going to learn more about as you continue reading this book). Like all Intuitives, I simply marched to the beat of my own drum.

I would not be here today writing my second book if I hadn't taken a long, painful, hard look at my life and made some incredibly difficult choices to change. We all need a time in our lives to truly figure out who we are. I hope this is your time. Please don't think I for one minute claim to have life and business all figured out now; my friends and family can certainly attest to the fact that I don't. I will always be a work in progress. I had to shift some things in my life to truly figure out who I am and what I am meant to be doing in this world. Only then could I finally start being unapologetically who I am in the world, especially in my business. I want the exact same things for you, which is why I wrote this book.

I have to give you a warning. This book is designed and written for go-getters who are intuitive, creative entrepreneurs. Whiners and complainers are not allowed. Why? Because this book contains detailed information on how you can start Living Your Life from the Front Seat and stop doing stuff you suck at. This book does not contain vague, general ideas. It's full of specific ways for you to truly start doing what you are good at in this world. You're going to have to listen to me and not make excuses. I hate excuses.

So before you read any further, I want you to ask yourself the following questions:

Are you committed to:

- letting go of all your excuses?
- doing what it takes to change your life?
- hearing and learning something new?
- finishing this book—reading the whole thing? (I know you have books sitting on your nightstand you started, but didn't finish.)

Are you ready to:

- do whatever it takes to build your business?
- put your business above laundry and running errands?

Are you willing to do something different? Since you're reading this book I'm guessing that what you are currently doing is *not* working.

If you are truly ready, I am really, really excited for you to start this journey of learning what it means to start Living Your Life from the Front Seat and stop doing stuff you suck at. Saying yes has put the Universe in motion to help you along the way.

Ok, I think you get the idea of what you are getting yourself into. Let's do this!

INTRODUCTION

This book is for those who want to live outside the confines of what society tells them they need to or should being doing with their life. It is for entrepreneurs who are creative and alive and want to set the world on fire with their ideas. I must admit I started this book thinking it would be for corporations, but I quickly realized that even though I speak to many corporate audiences each year, it is not necessarily where my passion lies. My passion lies with entrepreneurs and those who you will soon learn are called Intuitive Types. There is a lot of talk out there right now about this specific Myers-Briggs type that has a high propensity for entrepreneurship, which is 100% true. I am going to teach you exactly what being an Intuitive Type is all about. No more guessing or speculating. I am going to show you through Myers-Briggs why some people are more likely to become entrepreneurs and others are perfectly comfortable doing the 9-5 thing. We are made completely differently. One is not better than the other; we are simply different.

Some of you Intuitive Type people have already started your own businesses or you are doing what you *love* inside a company that allows you to do things your own way. But many of you are still stuck in corporate jobs you despise. This book is for all of you. I will show you why you are special, unique, and brilliant in this world (for real), and I will give you specific ways to become successful in whatever venture you decide to tackle.

I respect companies willing to bring in someone like me to ruffle the feathers of the status quo and be a truth-teller. They actually want their employees to be in positions that match their innate talents and passions, which sometimes means letting people go or finding others a new position that fits their creative soul. Only then can magic happen—when employees are happy and the company reaps the rewards 1000 times over. It is win/win in the best possible way.

When I speak to corporations, my favorite people in the room are the ones I can see having Aha! moments and saying, "Oh, *this* is why I hate my job...which is sucking the life out of me."

In my business, I surely don't want unhappy employees working for me. Having compassion for your people is essential, and a huge part of being a compassionate employer is wanting your people in the right positions that align with their innate skill set. This book is all about guiding you to make that happen. It is for the CEO, COO, manager, team leader, and employee who is open minded and willing to think outside the box and make some changes. It's for compassionate leaders.

This book is NOT for those who are simply surviving day-to-day and actually ok doing so. I don't work with those kinds of people anymore because I find it one of the saddest things in life. We only get one life on this earth and if you are willing to settle for just ok—just surviving—this book is NOT for you. Keep reading if you are a badass, cool, awesome person who wants to spend the rest of your life doing epic shit, being happy, fulfilled, and thriving every day. Can I get a hell yeah?

I can't tell you how many people I work with who allow the doubt of others to stop them from living their dreams. Have you heard things like:

- You can't quit your job! What will you do about health insurance? (They have individual plans, people.)
- What about your 401K? (They have freakin' IRAs, people.)
- That is really risky. Are you sure you want to do that? (Yes!)

- I really don't think anyone is going to buy that. (I'll find out.)
- This is going to take you years to build. Are you sure you want to do this? (Watch me.)
- What do you know about marketing? (I will learn.)

My hope is this book finally gives you permission to do whatever you want to do with your life because guess what? It is your life! I don't know about you, but I want to use my time on this earth to do the absolute most I can with it. Do you long to have more fun, be creative, wake up early because you can't wait to tackle the day, travel, help people, be powerful, laugh more, change lives, connect, speak your truth, do the work you're meant to do, and leave a legacy for your family?

Do you want to say whatever you want, do whatever you want, whenever you want? I know I do, which is why I work my butt off to own my own business. You direct sellers, entrepreneurs, and world-changers should be feeling a tingle in your spine…because I know you want it too.

If this sounds attractive to you, I promise you are going to enjoy this book—and it might even change your life. When I realized I was an Intuitive Type weirdo and stopped questioning it (and stopped letting *others* question it!), I truly started to embrace the fact that my weirdness is part of what makes me awesome. That's when my entire life changed.

I realize I may be alienating 75% of the population writing this book only for Intuitive (entrepreneurial) Types (as they are only 25% of the population) but this has to be said! You need to hear that there is nothing wrong with you. I want you to stop questioning yourself as I did for so many years. You are different from most people. I'm going to show you that your differences are awesome and key to setting you and your business apart.

Not only is it ok to be different, it is how God designed you. God designed each and every one of us; that is a fact. You were born into this world with your personality. Did you know that? Our type is innate! Life circumstances can affect or seemingly change your type, but that doesn't really happen. Your type does not change throughout your lifetime and you'll learn all about that as we continue together in this book.

When I started living the way God designed me to live everything got easier. I like to think of it as a little tap on the butt by God when we start taking the steps towards the life we are supposed to be living. Do you know the feeling that something else is in store for you and you just have to figure out what it is? Well, that is God nudging you. He doesn't give us ideas we aren't supposed to have.

This book will give you clear direction using the work by Isabel Briggs Myers and her mother Katherine Briggs, the creators of Myers-Briggs Type Indicator. I use this powerful assessment with all my clients; it is the foundation for everything. In addition, I share what I've learned from my amazing teachers—personal and business coaches, other authors, professional colleagues, and my clients.

You might be getting the idea that this business book is not written for just anyone. You're right. It is written for entrepreneurs or want-to-be entrepreneurs. I want to sincerely and wholeheartedly thank the Sensors and the 9-5'ers, because without them our society would fall apart. They literally help the world go 'round. We are two different kinds of people, innately, and that is OK. I will show you how and why we are different throughout this book and I hope that once and for all you see the difference, accept it, and move on with your life. Stop trying to be like everyone else, trying to fit into someone else's mold that isn't for you. I want you to design our own life based on your innate personality type. Once you do that, things can finally start to fall into place and you can start living the life you are meant to be living.

The first step in designing your Front Seat Life is to answer these three amazing questions:

Who are you?
Where are you going?
How are you going to get there?

In order to get clear about your business, attract your ideal clients, and make money, you must get to know yourself. Only then can you offer a product or service aligned with something you are innately good at. I believe this is the missing piece for so many people. They try to build a business on what they think others may want or need. Yes, we need to know our ideal client, but first you must build your business upon something you were born into this world to do. If you want flow in your life, go on this journey with me about learning who you are. Once you know who you are, you can go about designing your life and your business.

You Intuitive Types must do things your own way based on how you were made. You need to design your lives, not let life design it for you. In order to attract your ideal clients, you must start with yourself. Quit trying to get everyone to like you. They aren't going to so get over it. If you are being vanilla, not taking a stand for what you believe, nobody will know how to find you.

Think about it: when you are looking for a real estate agent, a therapist, a coach, or a photographer, you ask your friends for a referral or you might even post an inquiry on Facebook. Typically, you have a specific (not a general) need. Not just anyone will do. You want to know their specialty, their niche. Your personality is the start of all that. It is such a waste of your precious time and energy trying to get everyone to like you, trying to fit to everyone else's mold. Instead I am asking you to figure out who you are and attract the right people to you. My BHAG (Big Hairy Audacious Goal) is to get everyone to start living according to who they are, not who other people want them to be. Attract—not chase! This alone will change your life, so are you ready to get started on discovering *you*?

I have spent the past four years since my divorce and the last two-and-a-half years since my first book, *Live Your Life from the Front Seat*, doing personal inventory and working on myself and my business. I have been through everything I share in this book. I'm on a lifelong journey, not a specific destination, and I am far from perfect coming to you today. But I know these principles I am going to teach you work because they have worked for me and thousands of clients over the past many years. All of us are always a work in progress. I like to say we're all evolving. So reading this book is likely going to be step one for you—the awareness phase—which is fantastic because no change can happen until we first have awareness.

Some of the learning in this book will be challenging for you, but I *know* if you embrace it and accept the truth, it will change your life and your business forever. The changes you desire will not happen overnight, but I hope this book will be a guide to you on your discovery of yourself—the good and the not so good.

Who Are You? Understanding Who You Are Innately

I have chosen to start by discussing personality Types because it is critical. It is the foundation of this book because personality type is innate and the basis of everything we are going to discuss. It is the very start of the process of coming to understand who you are. The reason I do this is because I know understanding your own personality type can help tremendously with:

- building awareness of individual differences.
- enhancing your understanding of yourself and others.
- appreciating your own and others' strengths and gifts.
- knowing your own and others' personality types, which provides a language and a framework for effective understanding and communication.

Once we have uncovered your innate personality type using the MBTI basics, I will introduce my own unique way of incorporating it into your life; I call it Living Your Life from the Front Seat. It is designed to help you understand your type in a way that allows you to use it for the rest of your life because I know it can and will change your life. It will help you understand yourself and your relationships in a new and powerful way.

We will also dive deep into the areas where you and your team excel, and what you suck at and need to avoid. We will explore what happens during stressful times so you can identify this in yourself and those you work with, giving you deeper compassion and an ability to get everyone back on track. Sounds awesome, doesn't it? Living Your Life from the Front Seat is awesome.

Where Are You Going?
Up-Leveling Your Mindset

Many of you may not even be aware of your mindset or what mindset even is. We are going to spend the third section of this book digging deep into your current mindset and how you can exponentially up-level it to get all the things you desire in your life and business.

How Are You Going to Get There?
Taking Action! Three S Method™

As important as our mindset is, none of that matters if we are not taking consistent action toward those goals we are going to set. I will introduce you to my Three S Method™ focusing on structure, systems, and singular focus.

So are you with me? Do you want to discover who you are, where you are going, and how you are going to get there? Are you ready to learn about your innate talents, stop doing stuff you suck at, up-level your mindset, stop making excuses, and really start taking action in your life? If so, this book is for you. Let's do this.

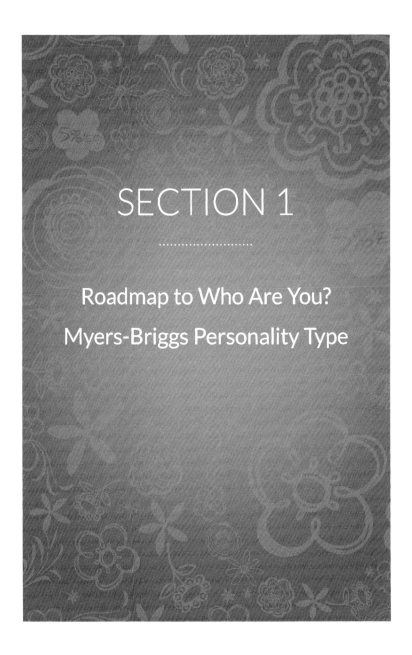
SECTION 1

Roadmap to Who Are You?
Myers-Briggs Personality Type

CHAPTER 1

Nature vs. Nurture

*"Don't chase people; attract them.
Just show up and do your thing;
the right people will show up and stay."*

—UNKNOWN

Alright, let's start by telling the truth: you are messed up in some way, so am I, and it is totally normal and perfectly ok. God designed you perfectly but society, your family, someone or something has ruined that perfection. Being a therapist for many years, I know this to be true 100% of the time. Everyone is damaged in *one way or another.* What I am interested in is helping everyone understand the limiting beliefs (put upon you by someone else) which may be keeping you from doing what you are meant to be doing in this world. I want you to then embrace your innateness so you can start living the life you were meant to live. If I would have stayed stuck in the limiting belief that I can't write based on almost not passing my thesis in graduate school, I never would have written this book (or the one before it). I had to choose to believe that "I'm a bad writer" was not true, but was circumstantial at the time. We can all grow and evolve so don't let some limiting belief keep you from doing something you want to do.

However, I did have to write based on my personality type and my own unique way of doing things. I have a confession to make. My first book was a hard process and I was still holding onto the *shoulds* that society has for authors, psychotherapists, and books. *Shoulds* like: you shouldn't swear, it should be written in a scholastic manner, it should help everyone, your cover should look more professional, and it shouldn't be so conversational. I believed that so much at the beginning that I hired a ghostwriter to help me. She took my ideas and wrote large sections of the book for me.

I will never forget the day I got her draft back. I sat down on my floor at my coffee table with a cup of coffee, and started reading. Within minutes I was filled with tears and anger. What I was reading was a boring, vanilla, edited version of my thoughts and beliefs. There was no "me" in it at all—none. I had an Aha! moment right then and there. I realized nobody can teach the way I teach, nobody can write the way I write, and nobody can coach the way I coach. The exact same thing is true for you. You don't have to do things their way; you get to do things your way and nothing feels better than that. Not everyone is going to like it, but that is actually a good thing. You can weed out the people who don't like your videos, your writing, your website, or your marketing materials long before they call you to work with you. You only want to attract the ideal clients, not everyone. That was a lesson in limiting beliefs I had to crush in order to move on.

So, I want you to really think about some of your limiting beliefs in this next section about nurturing because those beliefs are affecting your life and business much more than you likely realize.

Think of this illustration as we go along.

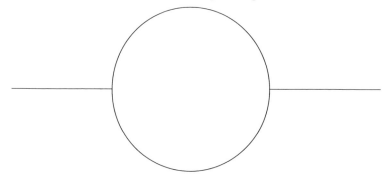

The line on left is how you were born into this world and who you were as a child. Were you nerdy, introverted, fun, creative, outgoing, shy, funny, goofy, talked to everyone, had only a few friends, had lots of friends, played well with others or preferred to play alone? Think for a moment about who you were as a child. In the space below, write down some thoughts, images or adjectives that you think describe you as a child.

_____

_____

_____

_____

_____

The large circle in the middle represents all the stuff that happens and the people who influence us as we grow up.

- School
- Teachers
- Parents
- Friends
- Siblings
- Culture
- Neighborhood
- College
- Naysayer or bully trauma
- Abuse

This stuff shapes who we are much more than we can even imagine, and here's the kicker: most of it is complete bullshit and/or doesn't even belong to us. But we take it on as if it IS.

Now take a moment to think about (and write down) some of the limiting beliefs that have been placed upon you that may be holding you back from your brilliance in your work.

There is an amazing book called *The Four Agreements* by Don Miguel Ruiz. You must add it to your reading list. One of the four agreements we need to make with ourselves is that we can't take anything personally. That agreement has changed my life and is so true when we are dealing with our pasts. Most of those things that were said or done to you have NOTHING to do with you. They have to do with that other person. There are good people that mean well that still mess us up (99% of the parents out there) and then there are just jerky people. Either way, we usually don't own any of that garbage.

This book is about showing you how to show up unapologetically as who you are, while being a good person and not taking on the judgments of what other people think. This work is imperative for the success of your life and business and clearly I am only introducing it here. If you feel like you need to do more work to identify your limiting beliefs, seek out an excellent therapist or alternative healer to help you uncover the issues put on you by others. I still see someone regularly and it has helped my life and business tremendously.

What we are going to be doing over the following pages is to help you get back to that innate child in you—who you were before the world got ahold of you and molded you into the person they thought you *should* be. My goal is to get you back to *you*!

Nature:
Myers-Briggs Type

"The thing that is really hard, and really amazing, is giving up on being perfect and beginning the work of becoming yourself."

—ANNA QUINDLAN

Ok, we are past the yucky stuff for now, I promise. Now we get to spend many chapters discussing your awesome innateness and how God designed you.

I love the Myers-Briggs Type Indicator. As I mentioned before, it is my favorite tool to help you figure out who you are. Type is innate, meaning all of us were born with our type. I believe God gave you your type and your personality for a reason. We are all meant to be who we are. Wouldn't you agree that doing things the way God designed you is easier than trying to become great at something else? Yes, we all work on things to improve ourselves but when I do what God designed me to do, life is easier. We are going to spend the rest of this book discussing how to design your business around your innateness, but first we have to learn what that is.

As we begin the self-assessment you will inevitably think of others in your life, but try first to put on your own oxygen mask and then come back around a second, third, or twelfth time to assess your family and/or coworkers. Let go of who you think your spouse wants you to be, or who your parents thought you should be, or what your job requires you to be.

Many authors suggest this same concept in their books, but the missing piece is an actual tool to help you figure out exactly what those things are. The Myers-Briggs Type Indicator is that tool.

It is important for you to understand a little bit of background on type. If you're an Intuitive Type like me, you might be tempted to jump past this seemingly boring stuff, but I promise it is important. Fortunately, one of my unique gifts is to take boring concepts and make them relatable and fun, so stick with me.

Background

Here are some important foundational points to understand about type:

- Type is based on solid research.
- Type does not change, but life circumstances change.
- We have a preference.
- There is a scale of preference.

What is Type?

First things first: What is type and where does it come from? I know, I know, this is boring for you Intuitive Types, but I have made it short because it is important to understand. (You Sensing and Thinking Types will love this.)

The Myers-Briggs Type Indicator has its roots in the works of Carl Jung, a famous Swiss psychologist who talked about archetypes and how we understand ourselves through them. In the 1940s, Isabella Myers and her daughter, Katharine Cook Briggs, took what Jung had described as archetypes and developed the Myers-Briggs Type Indicator. The MBTI has since become the most widely used personality assessment tool in the world. This is the original and most useful tool I have ever found to help people understand their innateness. The power of the MBTI is why I am spending my life teaching it and developing my own way of helping people understand it.

Type Does Not Change

There is always someone who wants to arm-wrestle me over this topic, but personality type is innate; it does not change. Your life circumstances change, but your type doesn't. Let me say that again.

Your type does not change, but your life circumstances change.

While you may think you were different in your youth than you are today, it wasn't your personality that changed—only your circumstances.

Life circumstances are things such as our family of origin, our school, our community, or the norms of society. Each tells us we're *supposed* to be a certain way, which may not enable our own strengths or types.

As children, we are who we are. We can be gregarious, or shy and reserved. We can be serious or playful. This is an example of our innate nature. It's important, when you think about yourself as we work through this next section, to do your best to remember yourself as you were in your childhood. You want to get back to the person you were intended to be, the person God created to bring your amazing gifts, talents, and self to be in the world.

Over time, and through the influence of those around us, we start to change to try and fit into a certain mold. We try to work better within a society and within our families. Sometimes the roles we are asked to take on are not ones in which we feel strongest, happiest, and healthiest.

You are meant to be a luminary, to shine light on this world, to share your God-given talents, and to be sustained by them. If you have picked up this book you're ready to bridge the gap between who you are innately and where you are now. I believe you found this book because you are ready, now, to do this work. I want to guide you back to who you are innately so you are living your best life and attracting the right clients.

We Have a Preference

Handwriting Example

Take a moment and do a little something for me in the space below. First, write your name with your dominant hand on the first line. How did that feel? Write down how that felt.

_____

_____

_____

Now repeat this exercise with your non-dominant hand.

_____

_____

_____

Write how it felt to use your non-dominant hand.

_____

_____

_____

If you're like most people, when you wrote with your dominant hand it felt:

- comfortable
- natural
- easy
- confident
- strong
- second nature
- effortless

Alternately, when you wrote with your non-dominant hand, chances are you said it felt:

- awkward
- sloppy
- challenging
- child-like
- uncomfortable
- required extra effort

I trust you are smart people (since you are reading this book), so you probably understand why I had you do this exercise. I did this because I wanted to illustrate a point. Everyone has a type which is just like that handwriting exercise. Everyone is able to write with either hand, some to greater or lesser ability than others. The same holds for personality Type. While we may have a greater or lesser preference for doing things a certain way, we always have a preference.

If someone was to throw a ball at your face, you would try to catch it with your dominant hand 100% of the time; it would be second nature to you. Your type preference is like this example—you *could* catch the ball and write your name with either hand, but you always have a preference for the dominant hand or your preferred Type.

Scale of Preference

The Teeter-Totter

Imagine yourself standing on a teeter-totter. Standing in the middle, you have one foot on each side of the teeter-totter. As you imagine yourself walking to one side or the other, at some point the end you're standing on is going to drop to the ground.

This is a visual of what it looks like to have a slight preference (in the middle) and a strong preference (way at one end).

- 1–5 is a slight preference.
- 5–10 is a little stronger.
- 10–20 is a clear preference.
- 20–30 is a strong preference.

In the middle of the teeter-totter, you are close to both sides of the spectrum, and therefore can understand both dichotomies and can also relate well to both. But remember the handwriting example, you still always have a preference—even if it is slight.

As you move toward the seats, you are much farther away from the other side, and therefore don't relate as well to the other dichotomy. As we go through the self-assessment in the next section, imagine where you think you may fall on that scale of 1–30. Are you in the middle of the teeter-totter with a slight preference (1–5)? Or are you in middle with a clear preference (6–15)? Or are you at the end with a very strong preference (16–30)?

Something interesting can occur when we are looking at where we fall on the scale of preference in comparison to others in our lives. I have often seen Extroverts think they can't be an Extrovert because in comparison to their spouse or colleague who is a strong Extrovert (25–30 on the scale), they assume they must be an Introvert. That is not true.

I have two clients this has happened to:

> *The first was a married couple who owned and ran a business together. She was an extreme type, 25–30 on every dichotomy. They had been married for 20 years and were raising their four children. He had been functioning as her exact opposite type, and they both assumed he was until we typed him. Lo and behold, he turned out to be the exact same type as his wife, just not as strong as she was. Because she was so extreme in her preferences, he assumed he couldn't also be that type, and had been taking on all the functions in the family as his opposite type—and HATED it! He was exhausted, resentful, and sad. Since our work together, he has changed jobs, and they have hired people to do the activities in their business they both suck at. They have so much more time and energy for each other, their business, and their amazing kids.*

Just because someone close to us is stronger on the scale doesn't mean we can't also be on that scale. It can certainly make us question ourselves, but this is not about comparing to others, it is about being who we are.

There is no judgment in being who you are. You are who you are.

In this next section, we're going to use those teeter-totters to explore the different pairs of the Myers-Briggs assessment tool so you can conduct your own self-assessment and figure out who you are. This will help you get to know who your best self is so you can move forward in your life and business.

Don't Put Me in a Box

There is always someone who says they don't like personality assessments because they don't like to be put into a box. Well, coming from someone who makes a living thinking outside the box, I don't like that either—trust me!

I am no mathematician, but with four different dichotomies, a scale of preference from 1–30, and our uniquely nurtured selves (family of origin, birth order, traumas, culture of origin), no two people can be exactly alike. One type is not going to look exactly like another type, but there are similarities and it is just as important to understand how and why we are like some people and not like others. Myers-Briggs is the best tool I have ever found for that kind of discovery.

So, if you are one of those doubters and have gotten this far, please stick with me; you won't regret it. I will show you plenty of *outside of the box* thinking, I promise.

The Dichotomies/Pairings

I used to do a radio show with a colleague where we talked each week about type. She hated when I used the word "dichotomies," and told me I needed to dumb it down and use a word we all knew. We came up with "pairing." While I was trained to use the word dichotomy, I realize many of you may have the same reaction she did, so I will use both words interchangeably.

The MBTI is all about understanding who we are. The four pairings (or dichotomies) by Myers and Briggs are just the beginning of this amazing work, but an essential piece since everything builds on this foundation.

Each dichotomy (set of opposite pairs) deals with different parts of our personality. There are four dichotomies: Extrovert/Introvert (E/I), Sensor/Intuitive (S/N), Thinking/Feeling (T/F), and Judging/Perceiving (J/P). Each dichotomy deals with a separate part of our psyche. (Myers and Briggs already used I for Introvert, so please notice that they use the letter N for Intuition.)

The first (Extrovert/Introvert) is all about where you get your best energy. The second (Sensor/Intuitive) is about how you take in information. The third (Thinking/Feeling) is about how you make decisions. The fourth (Judging/Perceiving) is about how you like your world to be organized.

Let's jump in and get started with this modified MBTI self-assessment, which will help you figure out who you are and how to rock your business.

The dichotomies are fascinating by themselves, but the work gets much deeper after we build this important foundation. Each can teach you so much about yourself, relationships, and business.

It's worth repeating: we always have a preference and it is going to be important to answer these sections from your most true self—who you are at your core. If you are starting this book rather lost or broken (as most of us are), this may take some time to flesh out and that is OK. I suggest going through this section with some self-compassion and honesty. Try not to answer these sections with who you *should* be or who your family *thinks* you should be or how your boss or spouse *wants* you to be. Answer based on who *you really are*!

So, let's get started; it is going to be fun!

CHAPTER 2

Introversion and Extroversion

"Spend your free time the way you like, not the way you think you're supposed to"

—SUSAN CAIN

Most everyone has heard of Introverts and Extroverts. However, this is often the most difficult pairing for people to choose from.

There is also some talk about Ambiverts, which is when someone feels they truly cannot choose between whether they have a preference for Introversion or Extroversion. While I appreciate this can be a difficult choice for many people, you always have a preference, and I will show you why it matters as we continue and get into the *Live Your Life from the Front Seat* section. You have to choose! The section on your Back Seat will help you identify your preference for Introversion or Extroversion when you identify where you go under stress. Before we continue, I want to address a few concerns I hear about choosing between Introversion and Extroversion.

The main reason people have a difficult time choosing is because we evolve as we grow older. While we always have the same preference for either Extroversion or Introversion, the scale of our preference may change. As a child, you most likely had a more extreme preference for either Introversion or Extroversion, but we live in the world with other people who influence our behavior (not our type). Introverts may find themselves liking to be around people more as they age/evolve, or Extroverts may realize they need more time alone, since they give so much of themselves to the world. Our preference has not changed, but the strength of it on the scale of 1–30 may lessen.

Up until my late 20s, I was a 28 on the scale of Extroversion. As I have grown older, I have simply learned to enjoy being alone. It doesn't mean I am now an Introvert. I am more like a 20 on the scale and I have learned to enjoy time by myself—journaling, traveling, reading, and walking in nature. It brings me peace in my 40s that I couldn't experience in my 20s.

As we go along, I will be sharing my unique take on type that I have curated over the past 20 years while working with clients. There are many books out there that are just about the facts of type, but I find them rather boring and clinical. While I will share some facts, I have also broken down each section into unique areas I hope will help you see each dichotomy in a new way to help you find your truest type.

Now, back to Extroversion and Introversion.

The first dichotomy has to do with energy—where you give and get your best energy. Introverts and Extroverts are energized in different ways, and people are either Extroverts (E) or Introverts (I), some to a greater extent than others (remember the teeter-totter). You can range from 1–30 on the scale.

Extroverts give their best energy to the world. They're energized by their outer world. They focus on people and things. They're typically active. They have many interests and often have many friends. Extroverts are external processors; they think aloud. There's no hidden best part of an Extrovert because they give that best self away to the world around them. Doing this energizes them and makes them happy.

Introverts, on the other hand, are energized by their inner world. They get energy and recharge from being alone. Introverts save their best self for themselves. They're focused on concepts and ideas and are typically reflective. Introverts have few interests, but know them deeply. Likewise, they have few friends, but a deep connection with those whom they allow close to them. It takes time to get to know an Introvert and what is in his/her heart, and they show the world their second-best self. When an Introvert runs a company, she will do it best if she is aware of how much time she needs to recharge.

In the workplace, almost all of us have to show up as Extroverts so often that Introverts, especially those in managerial roles, have to use most of their extroverted energy to help them get through the day. When I work with teams, the team is almost always shocked to learn their CEO or manager is an Introvert. Understanding type in all areas of our lives can allow us to be more of who we naturally/innately are and to quit wasting our precious energy.

Here are some common words to describe Introverts and Extroverts. Circle the words that you think best describe you.

Introvert	Extrovert
Energized by inner world	Energized by outer world
Focus on concepts, ideas	Focus on people, things
Reflective depth of interest	Active
Understand it before live it	Lots of different interests
Inwardly directed	Live it, then understand it
	Outgoing

I have been working with type for over 20 years, and through that time I have come up with some unique ways to describe type that help people really get it. I hope the following sections help solidify your preference for introversion or extroversion.

Where We Give Our Best Self

Imagine that you own a long-sleeved shirt with a heart painted on the sleeve, and think of the saying "wearing your heart on your sleeve." This relates to how some people show and give themselves to the world.

Extroverts wear the heart facing out to the world. As you walk around, everyone can see the heart. In everything you do, you show people yourself. Your every gesture shows everyone who you are. Extroverts show and give their best self to the world. It is visible to the outside world just like the heart on the outside of your sleeve.

Introverts wear that heart on the inside of their sleeve. The world does not see the Introvert's best self. They hide that best self and keep it for themselves and those close to them. Someone has to get very close to you in order to see your true self, which is hiding on the inside of your sleeve.

With Others

One of the biggest differences between Extroverts and Introverts is how they interact with people, most certainly their work colleagues.

Introverts have a hard time in large groups; the small talk is tiring and difficult for them. They much prefer to have a one-on-one conversation so they can go deeper with that one person. I have worked with countless Introverts that say small talk is literally painful for them. It isn't that they don't like or want to be social, but large parties or meetings where they are required to make small talk are not fun or interesting for them.

Extroverts, on the other hand, get their energy from being with people. Being social and with other people gives them energy and since they are naturally good at it, they enjoy it.

Introverts are usually better digging deep with a few clients while Extroverts usually prefer one to many, which includes coaching a group or educating/training larger groups. My book coach

Karen Lynn Maher and I are a good example of this difference: I prefer to speak to groups when I'm training and she thrives in the one-on-one environment.

External and Internal Processing

When I describe Introverts and Extroverts, I often talk about how these two types process information. Each type takes in information in their own way and then processes it through different filters.

Extroverts are *external* processors. They often talk before they think. They process information externally. Extroverts live it, then understand it. When they are given new data or information, they talk their way through it. If there is a problem in their life (or in someone else's life), Extroverts prefer to work things out in an external way. They might write an email, post something to Facebook or Instagram, draw something, dance or sing or do something physical to help them process the information they have gathered. They work through things outside of their heads. Whatever is easiest and closest, Extroverts tend to use it to work through their current issue/challenge.

Introverts are *internal* processors. They process information before they say it, write it, draw it, or do anything with it. An Introverted person tends to be quiet, and to take in a lot of information before they are ready to form an opinion, or make a decision and speak their mind. Because they take the time to process information before making a statement or contributing to a conversation, Introverts often go unheard in meetings. They often don't get a chance to add to the conversation and the decision-making process unless there are many other Introverts in the organization.

Extroverted World

The biggest challenge for Introverts, particularly in America, is that we live in a strongly extroverted world. Extroversion is rewarded. The person who is involved in a large variety of activities is perceived as being successful. They are the ones running the world. So much of what we do is rewarded by what we are perceived to be doing. It's important for us to understand that Introverts need to process information differently than the other half of the population. Again, there is not a right and wrong type, but there are *marginalized* types. Introverts are the first marginalized type since we live in such an extroverted world.

If there is a meeting that is going to happen, the Extrovert is normally the one who is putting together the agenda, deciding who is going to do what, determining topics to be discussed, and running the meeting. They go from one point to another in rapid-fire sequence, not pausing to see if anyone has anything to add or ask at the time.

One thing we need to learn about each other is we take in information in different ways and at different speeds. Extroverts think and speak on the fly. Introverts need time to process information. Their filter is determining what they want to say at an appropriate time. This means they need more time to get out their thoughts and feelings.

Extroverts sometimes need to stop talking to let the Introverts talk. Introverts need to find the courage to say, "I need to be heard." Knowing this can help us to communicate better in our relationships and businesses. If we don't take time to listen to Introverts, we're losing out on hearing from them. External processing doesn't make Extroverts more correct; it just makes them more vocal.

What Others Have to Say

As you can well imagine, some character traits of one type often cause stress for the other type. When I recently ran a workshop with a corporate client, I divided the groups into their natural types, and asked each type (the Introverts and the Extroverts) several different questions including how they perceived the other type, and what they wanted the other type to know about them. The results of those discussions gave me a lot of insight into both types.

What others have to say...

Extroverts About Introverts

When Extroverts were asked how they perceived Introverts, they said they perceive Introverts as being:

- Selfish
- Hiding
- Quiet
- Shy
- Hard to know
- Individualistic
- Slow to communicate
- All about them
- Have a dull life
- Rigid
- Mysterious
- Boring
- Easy to be alone
- Sensitive
- Pansies
- Thoughtful
- Dependable
- Reliable
- Loving
- Great listeners
- Inflexible
- Loyal
- Faithful
- Focused
- Careful
- Realistic
- Overthinking
- We are afraid you are lonely
- Want to shake you to know you are alive
- Slow

Introverts about Extroverts

On the other hand, when I asked Introverts how they perceived Extroverts, they said they perceive Extroverts as being:

- Loud
- Pushy
- Bold
- Overwhelming
- Impatient
- Impulsive
- Self-assured
- Playful
- More fun
- Unreserved
- Dismissive
- Obnoxious
- Too much
- Interesting
- Fascinating
- Exhausting
- Confident
- Powerful
- Unfiltered
- Squeaky wheel

"What I want you to know about me..."

Extroverts

During that same exercise at the workshop, I also asked each type what they would like the other type to know about them. These answers were typical of what many Extroverts say they want Introverts to know about them. Extroverts want you to know:

- We are exciting
- We want to know you
- We're outgoing
- We want to include you
- We're self-assured
- Forgive us for thinking out loud
- We really do want to hear you/include you
- We're expressive
- Our lack of filter isn't intended to hurt you
- We are loving, in a loud way
- We don't want to make you feel uncomfortable

Introverts

I did the same exercise with the Introverts at a company retreat, and this group shared with me what Introverts want you to know about them:

- We are smart
- You are intimidating
- We need time alone, but don't exclude us
- Invite me to participate
- Listen to me when I talk
- Show me you get me
- Patience
- Quiet
- Time
- Compassion
- Interested in what we have to say
- Value in the way we do things
- Thoughtful = good
- Drop the timer
- Give me space to be my best
- Give me a chance to think and talk
- Understanding
- Respect
- Connection
- Just because I'm quiet doesn't mean I don't care, that I'm dumb, or don't get it

Our Energy

Now that we have dug into our first dichotomy, Introversion and Extroversion, and I have shared how we are perceived, it is a great time to discuss being in congruence.

We must be aware of our own energy in our businesses so we know who we are attracting while still showing up and being unapologetically who we are. This is not about changing who we are. However, if you are not aware of how others are perceiving you, you may be confused as to who you are attracting as clients. A question I like to ask myself often (and one that I ask all my clients to consider) is, "How do you want people to experience you?" I would like to get these two things to a place of congruency: who you are and how your clients, employees, and others experience you. It is so much easier to just show up and be who you are than to fake it or try to be something you are not. So as we move forward, can we agree that who you are innately is also how you would like people to experience you?

Real Stories

Mary and David

The first example of the difference between Introversion and Extroversion is not necessarily a business example, but these therapy clients of mine are a perfect example of how these types can show up in a relationship. Mary and David came to see me last year because they were struggling to communicate, a trait shared by many of my clients. We did some initial work to assess what the issues were and get over some major humps. Then we did their personality assessments and the aha's started to happen.

David is a strong Extrovert. He likes to be around people, and he gets his energy from spending time with friends, talking, going out, being in nature, sharing happy hour, and talking with his wife. Mary, a strong Introvert, liked being alone a majority of the time. She enjoys silence and solitude after a long day at work. She could simply be in the same room with David and feel connected even though they were just watching TV, reading together, or on their own computers. She felt connected and like they were spending quality time together.

As we started to talk through this, David realized he did not have those same feelings—he felt isolated from Mary, often wondered what she was thinking, and wished they could be out doing something. As we spent a few weeks talking about their differences in this area, they learned how they could navigate their differences and compromise so they both could get their needs met within and outside of the relationship.

David felt guilty leaving Mary alone, which we soon realized was all made up in his head. Mary did not mind being left alone one or two nights a week to do her own Introverted things like reading, taking a bath, and doing research online for things she liked. David started doing things with friends a few nights a week to fulfill his need for interaction and activity.

They also started compromising on the things they did together on date nights. Mary was happy staying home, while David always wanted to go out. So while neither loved the other's plans, they did so happily knowing and understanding (for the first time ever) the importance of their differences and how they could make each other happy.

It was certainly a relationship-changing realization for Mary and David. Knowing and understanding their differences gave them language and a framework to start using so they could express their needs without hurting one another.

Karen and Jessica

My book coach Karen Lynn Maher and I are actually a great example of this dichotomy. Karen is an INFJ, and I am an ENFJ, and while we share many similarities in our NFJness, we differ greatly in where we like to give our energy and what brings us energy.

As an introverted entrepreneur, Karen prefers to work with clients one-to-one or in small, intimate groups. If she does a workshop, she also prefers it to be small and intimate. She has this preference because she gets and gives better energy in one-to-one relationships. Groups drain her so much that it is hard for her to keep her energy up, which is completely normal for most introverts.

I, on the other hand, prefer groups—and large groups, at that. It suits my extroverted energy to feed off the energy of large groups. Again, this is about energy. I feel energized in a crowd, while my energy gets drained when I spend too much time alone.

There is no right or wrong. It is just a preference, and we must know this in our businesses to best design the work we are doing with clients.

Which One Are You?

Extrovert or Introvert?

I hope I have given you enough detail to give you confidence to choose which type you have a preference for and to what degree (1–30). If you need a little extra help, you can also take the free assessment on my website at **www.jessicabutts.com**. Take a moment here to choose which one best describes you. Where do you think you fit on the Extrovert/Introvert scale? Are you strongly introverted? Are you strongly extroverted? Or are you somewhere in between? Draw where you think you are on that teeter-totter.

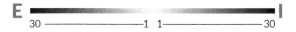

E ▬▬▬▬▬▬▬▬▬▬▬▬▬▬▬▬▬▬▬ I
30 ——————————1 1—————————— 30

CHAPTER 3

Sensing and Intuition

"Intuitive types are absolutely different and weird, and also totally awesome."

—JESSICA BUTTS

This is my favorite pairing because it has defined my entire life. Once you hear more about it, you may feel the same way. As I mentioned in the *Letter to My Readers* and my *Introduction*, I have always felt like a weirdo. I have always thought different, felt different and wanted more. It took me many years to realize that this part of my personality is the reason why I have always had these feelings. I now work almost exclusively with Intuitive Types to help them realize that their differences from the majority of the population are not a bad thing, but part of what makes them unique and special.

There is a lot of recent talk in the Myers-Briggs community, as well as with many entrepreneurial coaches, that there is indeed something that sets entrepreneurs apart from others. No more guessing or speculating on who those people are; they are Intuitive Types, plain and simple. This does not mean Sensors can't also be excellent entrepreneurs, but Intuitives are naturally designed that way. Once I realized this about myself, and when I help my clients see it in themselves, everything changes. We can quit thinking there is something wrong with us and finally start stepping into our innateness and go for it.

In this section, I will explain the huge differences in this dichotomy and how you can learn to understand them and embrace them, whether you are Sensing or Intuitive. Most people are not aware of how much this part of our innate personality affects our lives, our relationships, and how we feel about ourselves. Most everyone has heard about Extroversion and Introversion, but few people know about Sensing and Intuition and how important they are to understanding ourselves and the career we choose. Sensors are 9-5'ers and are totally fine with it. However, Intuitives are entrepreneurial and want to do things their own way. We must know this about ourselves before choosing a career. If you are reading this and know a teenager that is about to choose a major in college, please pass this book along to them or buy them a copy so they don't make the same mistake so many of us did by choosing the wrong career and spending years regretting it.

There is also a huge discrepancy in the division of people in this dichotomy. Sensors are 75% of the population and Intuitives are only 25%.

The dichotomy of Sensing (S) and Intuition (N) is about how we take in information. Sensors take in information through their five senses, and they are represented by the letter S. Intuitives, represented by the letter N, go more by gut and energy rather than facts.

Because Sensors validate information via their five senses, information is valid if they can touch it, taste it, hear it, smell it or see it. Sensors are very literal, concrete and factual. I say Sensors have an "internal file cabinet" because in their brains, they may remember how someone looked at them, the tone in their voice, or if they rolled their eyes at them. Sensors live in the here and the now. They are happiest now, and aren't always looking to what's next. Strong Sensors are big on routine, and the 9-5. They tend to take things literally and live in the moment. Remember, Sensors make up 75% of the world's population! Yes, 75%. They are "gotten" by most people since 3/4 of the population are like them. Most people are Sensing Types, and therefore, they can relate to one another more easily.

Intuitives (N), the other 25% of the world's population, are what I call "future-thinkers" and "what-if 'ers." Where Sensors take in information with their five senses, Intuitive Types take in information via their "sixth" sense. Intuitive Types have an energetic vibe, gut feeling, a hunch, or a speculation about someone or something. Intuitive Types are more figurative than literal and prefer the big picture. They walk into a room and immediately get a vibe for what is going on. They just have a sense of something, so it's less specific and more about the bigger picture. Intuitive Types often think about what's next, and they need to dream and spend a lot of time imagining what could come next.

Here are a few key words to describe each type. Which words resonate with you? Circle the words that feel best to you.

Sensing	Intuition
Facts	Meanings
Data	Possibilities
Detail	Hunches, speculation, gut instinct
Reality-based	Theoretical
Here and now	Fantasy
Literal	Figurative

Choosing a Career

When choosing a career, the Sensing/Intuition dichotomy is the most important one to consider. How we are innately designed as either Sensor or Intuitive makes a huge impact on our satisfaction with our career long term.

Since 75% of the population is a Sensing Type, we can safely deduce that our world around us is largely designed for Sensors' characteristics and personalities. This is exactly why most Intuitive types don't fit in and need to pave their own path in their careers. Most 9-5, Sensing jobs make us want to pull our hair out. We are designed by God to do things differently, pave our own way... be a little different. All you Intuitive Types, I give you permission to start thinking outside the box and paving your own way either in a corporation or your own business.

Weirdos and the Regular World

There is a huge discrepancy in the population breakdown between Sensing and Intuitive Types.

I am confident that most of you reading this book are the weirdos—Intuitive Types. Why do I know this? Because I am one as well, and I know our type *very* well. We love personal development, we are always looking for the next greatest thing to learn about ourselves, we are never done learning, we are always striving for more, and we are very entrepreneurial. Intuitives are drawn to this book for the same reason I am writing it—we have a desire for more knowledge, more growth, and more personal development.

This is not to say that Sensing Types don't want this as well, but they are simply better at just "being," which most Intuitive Types envy. I have often said being an Intuitive Type is a blessing and a curse. While we love being creative and learning, it can be exhausting to rarely be satisfied with what is. While Sensors have an ability to just be, Intuitives are always thinking about what's next, and that can be exhausting.

Sensors have an amazing ability to deal with the day-to-day world that Intuitives have a hard time with since the world is designed more for Sensors. We Intuitive Types are a little weird. Am I right? Have you always felt a little different? Misunderstood? Me, too.

Please remember, there is no right or wrong type. I am simply calling it like it is, and in doing so, I hope it resonates with you more than if you had heard it in the past. My intention in being a little sassy and honest is so you will get it and start using it. As I have mentioned, understanding this and implementing it will change your life and business for the better.

Small Talk

Small talk to Intuitive Types can be exhausting. They want to talk about concepts and big picture ideas, and they enjoy deep conversations about theories and possibilities. Small talk at parties can seem frivolous and a waste of time—especially for Introverted Intuitive Types.

Sensors are much better at talking about details and facts that often come from small talk with coworkers or at parties.

Internal File Cabinet

Sensors have an internal file cabinet in their brains where they store details about people, places, and things they can recall years later! If someone rolled their eyes at them back in 1995, they have that stored in their memory banks for later and pull it out to use when necessary.

Sensors are also quite traditional when it comes to holidays, birthdays, and other special occasions. This also has to do with their "file cabinet" of a brain. They have experienced special occasions a certain way in the past and they prefer things to stay that way.

Funnel

Imagine a funnel. Intuitive Types take in information and live at the top of the funnel—big picture, big concepts, ideas; lots of space to dream, to think, to create future ideas. There is more space at the top of the funnel to think outside the box.

Sensors take in information and like to live at the bottom of the funnel—details, specifics, concrete ideas, here and now, more compact ideas.

Money is a great example of this funnel. Intuitive Types typically know they have enough money, but not usually the exact amount, whereas Sensing Types want to know exactly how much money they have. Big picture vs. details.

Here and Now vs. Future

This is one of the most important differences between Sensing and Intuitive Types.

Intuitive Types are always thinking about the future and what's next. I call them "*what-if'ers*. You will hear them say things like, "Honey, *what if* we moved the kids to Costa Rica for a year and sold coconuts on the beach? *What if* we went to Iceland this year? *What if* I quit my job and wrote a book? *What if* we move abroad for a year and let the kids experience other cultures? What if, what if, what if…?" Intuitive Types are also dreamers; they love to dream and play with all possibilities. Sometimes Ns don't even have to act on all of their dreams, but they still like to dream. It is actually essential to them; it is part of their makeup.

Intuitives have a hard time living in the moment. They are always thinking about what's next. Whether that be the next client or where their business is going. Their minds are almost always there and not here. Again, I call this a blessing and a curse as I love the dreamer in me but it also doesn't allow me to be present very often. I find myself extremely disappointed at times when things or people don't live up to my expectations as well.

Is this resonating with you? Did you think you were the only one? You are not alone; you are just an Intuitive type.

Sensors are in the moment most of the time. They live in the here and now, and have an ability to simply "be" that Intuitives do not.

These differences can, of course, cause many issues in relationships between Sensors and Intuitives.

Walking Into a Room

When walking into a room, Sensing and Intuitive Types will take in information differently.

Intuitive Types immediately get a sense of the energy of the room. They notice how the room looks, the lighting, the music, the energy of the people there.

Sensing Types scan the room for details: who is there, how people are standing, how someone looks at them when they enter the room, how people are dressed, and their body language. This is all specific, detailed information that helps them understand the environment they just walked into in a way they can process. And it goes into the file cabinet in their brain so they can use it later to make decisions or use their intuition with people. Yes, Sensing Types still have intuition, they just use it differently than Intuitive Types.

The word "intuition" seems to imply that Sensors don't have it, and that isn't the case. While Sensors don't always read energy the way that Intuitives can, they can have intuition, sometimes very strong intuition. Since Sensors take in information via their five senses, they use that to read situations to get an intuitive hit. They scan their environment (or a person) for specific cues to give them data for their intuition. They read body language, the environment, tone of voice, and eye movement.

A budding therapist reached out to me a few years ago, and after learning that her personality type was Sensing, she believed she would be a horrible therapist since she isn't an Intuitive. After talking for an hour or so, she realized that she did, in fact, have a strong intuition with her clients and in her life. She just took it in via her excellent skills of observation.

So you Sensors out there, don't fret. As a business person, you can develop and rely on your intuition.

Moneymaker

If you are an Intuitive Type, your intuition is one of your most valuable resources in business. Think about it: 75% of the population sees things in a linear way. You, however, see things in way that just comes naturally to you (but seems different and bizarre to them). You see patterns with money, people, things, or concepts.

They don't see that!

I remember when I sat with one of my first therapy clients and could clearly see what was happening in the pattern of her life due to similar circumstances in her past. I was thinking, "I can't say this because she must also see this" and I didn't want to have a "Captain Obvious" moment with one of my first clients. I quickly could tell that she couldn't see it (partly because we are all too close to our stuff to see it, but partly because she was a Sensor and she saw in the present moment). I bucked up and told her what I was seeing from a high level, top-of-the-funnel kind of way...and guess what happened? She was blown away. In that moment I realized two things:

1. Not everyone knows what I know. That doesn't make me any smarter; I just have different knowledge to share and so do *you*.
2. My big picture, pattern way of seeing things might be my real way to help people! So how does this work in your business?

Whether you are an architect, a real estate agent, a bookkeeper, a coach, or a teacher (it doesn't really matter the job or industry) you have something special to share and a way of seeing the world that 75% of the population doesn't. Don't hide it or waste it...highlight it! Scream it from the rooftops!

What others have to say...

Sensors About Intuitives

When Sensors were asked how they perceived Intuitives, they said they perceived Intuitives as being:

- Flakey
- Head in the clouds
- Goofy
- Not sensible
- Never present
- Always thinking about what's next
- Unhappy unless planning a trip
- Creative
- Artsy
- Different
- Has a good gut feeling for people

Intuitives About Sensors

On the other hand, when I asked Intuitives how they perceive Sensors, they said they perceive Sensors as being:

- Rigid
- Controlling
- Boring
- Too detail-oriented
- Needs to learn to go with the flow
- Good at day-to-day life stuff
- Better with money than themselves
- Dream killers
- Would like them to think outside the box

"What I want you to know about me..."

Sensors

During that same exercise, I also asked Sensors what they want Intuitive Types to know about them. These answers are what Sensors say they want you to know about them:

- We need details
- We need you to be specific
- We can be intuitive too; we just do it differently than you
- Respect my need for specifics
- I remember every eye roll
- Words are powerful to me; choose them carefully

Intuitives

What Intuitives want you to know about them:

- We need to be able to dream; let us
- We may or may not follow through on all our ideas, but we still like to have them and share them with you
- We are smart
- We don't always have details for you; we trust our gut
- Details and facts are hard for us
- Dreaming is more fun than day-to-day
- Just because we are always thinking about the future doesn't mean we don't like our lives
- We need to be creative

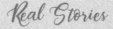

Nicole and Roger

Although this example is of a couple in therapy, it perfectly highlights the unique and complicated differences between Sensors and Intuitives.

Nicole and Roger came to me a few years ago, and they seemed to be deeply in love. As they started the session, they were affectionate and sweet with each other. I was curious to learn what issues would present themselves in our first session. Roger, as it turns out, was a strong Intuitive Type (30), and Nicole was a strong Sensing Type (27). Their issue, unbeknownst to them, revolved around this difference in their personality types.

Nicole started by telling me how she felt Roger didn't love her and their two children. He always seemed to be dreaming of the next best thing and never present in their day-to-day life. Roger talked often in their marriage about taking trips around the world with the kids, quitting their jobs and moving to Maui and getting simple jobs so they could eliminate some stress in their lives. Nicole viewed that as Roger wanting to run away from their life together with the children. But Roger wanted to do it together. Over the years, this began to create distrust and space between them. Once we discussed their types (and they realized that they both loved each other very much and wanted nothing more than to be together) we could talk openly about the differences between their innate personalities and work on some ways they could both be happy.

They worked out an agreement that during the week was day-to-day life, but on Wednesdays, Roger was able to go do something out-of-the-box. They started traveling more as a family, which gave Roger something to research, plan for, and look forward to. Nicole was able to **hear** Roger now that her feelings weren't being hurt by thinking he was unhappy in the marriage.

Erica and Jessica

My sister, Erica, and I are a great example of Sensing and Intuition. Erica is not only my sister, best friend, and all around awesome human being; she has also become my event assistant because she is awesome at it, being an ISFJ Type.

Erica and my two other assistants are both strong Sensing Types, and I wouldn't hire anyone otherwise. As a strong Intuitive Type, I have all the big ideas, so I don't really need any more help in that department. What I do need help with are the details, which Erica and most Sensors rock at.

Erica is good at being in the moment and attending to the details, while I can get lost in the idea of something new, fresh, and exciting. When I get lost in my dreams, Erica is great at bringing me back to reality.

I personally believe every Intuitive entrepreneur MUST have a Sensor as an assistant to help them with the stuff they suck at!

Erica and I simply take in information differently—and we need each other. She is a factual, concrete, details person, and I often have my head in the clouds and want to talk about the next idea before we are even done with our current event.

Sensing entrepreneurs need Intuitives to help them see the big picture since they can get lost in their heads and the weeds of the details and need an Intuitive to help them see the big picture. Again, there is no right and wrong type; we simply need to know our innate skills and what we suck at so we can balance each other out.

Which One Are You?
Sensing or Intuition?

I hope I have given you as much detail as you need to confidently choose which one you have a preference for and to what degree: (1–30). Take a moment here and choose which one best describes you. Where do you think you fit on the Sensing and Intuition scale? Are you strongly Sensing? Are you strongly Intuitive? Or are you somewhere in between? Mark yourself where you think you are on the scale.

S  N

30 ——————————1 1——————————30

CHAPTER 4

Thinking and Feeling

I am intrigued by marginalized types, and this dichotomy carries with it two different marginalized types: thinking women and feeling men.

This is the only dichotomy that is affected by gender, and it is also largely influenced by society. Roughly 75% of men are Thinkers and roughly 75% of women are Feelers.

The Thinking and Feeling dichotomy has to do with how we make decisions. The MBTI uses the letter T for Thinking and F for Feeling.

Once we've taken in our information through either Sensing or Intuition, we have to make decisions.

Thinkers make decisions with their heads. They like analysis. They like facts. They're objective and logical decision makers. This makes many Thinkers seem impersonal when it comes to decision making. It's not that they don't care about people; it's that they carefully analyze the pros and cons and make decisions that meet their criteria.

Feelers, on the other hand, primarily make decisions with their feelings. They also include everybody else's feelings if they might be affected by their choice. Each decision is made depending on the circumstances. This can cause a lot of conflict between individuals who make decisions in these different ways.

What's interesting is the challenge that male Feelers and female Thinkers experience in dealing with people who are the typical gender/type association in this personality type. Women who are Thinkers are often seen and categorized as bitches, and men who are Feelers are often seen and categorized as weak and indecisive. There is no judgment in being who you are. Simply accept that this is who you are, and learn how to work with others who are different from you. Here are some words that describe Thinking and Feeling:

Thinking	Feeling
Analysis	Sympathy
Objective	Subjective
Logic	Humane
Impersonal	Personal
Criteria	Circumstances

The Other 25%

With roughly 75% of women as Feelers and roughly 75% of men as Thinkers, that leaves only 25% of women as Thinkers and 25% of men as Feelers.

As with Intuitive Types, living your life as only 25% of the population can leave people feeling left out, misunderstood, marginalized, and as if they are on the outside looking in.

I enjoy working with marginalized types, and I find many of my female clients are Thinkers and many of my male clients are Feelers. Why? Because they have spent most of their lives feeling left out and not knowing why, until I explain Type to them. As we explore Type together, they start to understand these feelings of being different and left out. They can start to appreciate their uniqueness and rareness in this world.

Thinking women report feeling left out when around other women. They don't feel "gotten." They would rather spend time with men, and often find they have more male friends than they do female friends. Oftentimes when other women are sharing their feelings, it can make them feel uncomfortable and awkward. Because most Thinking women don't love what they consider to be the touchy-feely aspect of being female.

When I work with Thinking women who work primarily in a female-dominated industry, I encourage them to use their differences to their benefit. So if you are a direct seller, coach, or other female entrepreneur who works with other women, don't hide this; highlight it. Remember, don't chase people; attract them! Try it, and you will thank me! Even more importantly, you get to show up unapologetically as who you are, so it's a win/win.

Feeling men report similar experiences of feeling left out or misunderstood. They often don't "get" other men and other men don't "get" them. They prefer to have deeper relationships with women where they feel free to talk about their feelings.

Society's Role

Society tells little girls that they are *supposed* to be sweet and sensitive, want to sit around and talk about their feelings, and care about how everyone is feeling. But what if you don't? When you are born a Thinking woman, you likely felt a little different from an early age. You may have wanted to go play with the boys instead of playing house with the other little girls. As you can imagine, this can be quite confusing for little girls, and likely this has stuck around into adulthood.

Also, society tells men they are *supposed* to be tough, make difficult decisions, and not cry. But what if you do cry, are sensitive, and make decisions with your feelings as a man? Just like Thinking women, Feeling men feel different and left out. They grow up wondering if something is wrong with them.

My intention is for us to have a greater understanding of ourselves and others so we can stop labeling people as bitches or softies, understand we are all just born different, and then learn how to navigate relationships with all kinds of people in this world.

What others have to say...

Thinkers About Feelers

When Thinkers were asked how they perceive Feelers, they said that they perceived Feelers as being:

- Flakey
- Too emotional
- Too talkative
- Overly sensitive
- Shares too many feelings
- Can appear silly

Feelers About Thinkers

On the other hand, when I asked Feelers how they perceived Thinkers, they said they perceive Thinkers as being:

- Harsh
- Impersonal
- Without feelings
- Better decision makers
- Curt
- Short
- Too critical
- Uncaring
- Insensitive

"What I want you to know about me..."

Thinkers

I also asked Thinkers what they want Feeling Types to know about them. These answers are what Thinkers say that they want you to know about them:

- We have feelings
- We care
- We just make decisions with facts
- We need you to be a little more logical at times

Feelers

What Feelers want you to know about them:

- We have a lot of feelings, about almost everything
- Other people's opinions of us matter
- We value feelings
- Just because we make decisions with our hearts doesn't mean we aren't smart
- Value our feelings
- Ask us how we feel about things
- Our feelings aren't always logical and that needs to be OK

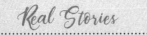
Real Stories

Feeling Man—James

James came to me quite a few years ago—broken, sad, and on the verge of being suicidal. He had spent his 35 years on this earth feeling different from all other men. He questioned his sexuality, his identity, and his manhood. After talking for a long time and hearing how much of his life revolved around typical "Thinking male" activities, we examined his type and discovered he was an extreme Feeling man (29 out of 30). As we talked about what it meant to be a Feeling man, how it felt, and the things he experienced as simply part of his type, he started to cry. For the first time in his life, he was seeing and understanding why he had felt different all these years. He knew from that moment on he needed to start embracing his Feeling side and likely needed to make some changes in his life. He was also able to cultivate this for his son who was also a Feeler. I can happily report he is doing well and living much more of his life from the Front Seat.

Thinking Woman—Kathy

Kathy, a female business owner, hired me a few years ago to coach her around her business. She knew she had a brilliant business idea, but it just wasn't taking off and she couldn't figure out why. Her product was made exclusively for women, which meant she needed to connect and sell to women. As we typed her in my office, we quickly realized she was an ENTJ, a strong Thinking woman (28 out of 30). The light bulbs started to go off for her. She realized the reason she was having a hard time selling her business idea to women is because she doesn't really connect to the majority (75%) of women. Her somewhat abrasive style was not attractive to most women. She is a brilliant idea-woman and is excellent at making things happen (her Front Seat), but she needed a Feeling saleswoman to help her connect with her ideal clients. She did just that and her business has been growing ever since. Now she gets to focus on the things she is great at.

> **Thinking and Feeling Coworkers—
> Farrah and Carrie**
>
> Farrah and Carrie are business partners whom I coach and counsel not only on their business model but also on their personality dynamics. Farrah is a strong Thinking woman (30 out of 30) and Carrie is a strong Feeler. This causes many issues in their working relationship. They are great friends who value their differences most of the time, but when they recently had to deal with a situation involving unclear compensation with a client, feelings got hurt. Farrah was 100% factual when it came to how she saw the compensation should be split based on who did the most work. Carrie, on the other hand, thought it should be split 50/50 regardless since they are friends and business partners. I helped coach them through how the other was feeling and they came to an agreement based on eventually seeing it through the others person's eyes, even if they didn't agree with it.

Which One Are You?
Thinking or Feeling?

I hope I have given you as much detail as you need to confidently choose which one you have a preference for and to what degree (1–30). So, take a moment and choose which one best describes you. Where do you think you fit on the Thinking and Feeling scale? Are you strongly Thinking? Are you strongly Feeling? Or are you somewhere in between? Indicate on the scale where you think you are.

T　　　　　　　　　　　　　　　　　　　**F**
　30 ─────────1　1─────────30

CHAPTER 5

Judging and Perceiving

The last dichotomy in the MBTI is Judging (J)/Perceiving (P). This has to do with how you like your world organized and how you like to be organized in the world. This is often the root cause of a lot of angst in a relationship, especially work relationships.

I love all the dichotomies for different reasons:

- E/I appeals to me because it helps clarify so much about communication.
- S/N is such a huge factor in so many Intuitives' lives to help them understand their differences in this world.
- T/F fascinate and intrigue me because if they fall into the minority 25%, they often feel misunderstood and left out.
- This last one, J/P, has such a huge influence on our way of being in this world, which dramatically affects our businesses.

The Boat Story

Many years ago, I had the divine pleasure of sailing the British Virgin Islands. While on the boat, I quickly realized I was one of only two Judgers. The other eight people on the boat were Perceivers.

I got up the first morning on the boat and went upstairs with everyone else to start our beautiful morning with coffee and breakfast. Before I could take my first sip of coffee, the J in me started asking all the normal J questions:

- What are we having for breakfast?
- What time is breakfast?
- Where are we going today?
- What islands will we be snorkeling at?
- Can you show me on a map?
- Where are we having lunch?
- What are we having for lunch?
- What are we doing after lunch?
- Are we getting off the boat today?
- If so, which island?
- What's fun on that island?
- Where are we having dinner?
- What time does the sun set?

I felt great and complete with the plan for the day. I could now relax into my day knowing the plan. Filled with contentment, I looked over at my friends...and their mouths had dropped to the floor in shock and horror as I had just ruined their day! Part of the fun for Ps, especially in an environment like a catamaran in the BVIs, is to let the day unfold as it comes. They wanted things to be spontaneous and to have *no* plan.

It was such a hilarious and poignant moment in my life that I tell this story at almost every workshop, because each type always has such an intense reaction. Js agree with me wholeheartedly and Ps usually look at me with disgust as I am telling this story.

The next morning, I still *needed* to know the plan but didn't want to ruin it for my P friends. I took the captain aside and asked all the same questions, but only *I* knew the plan for the day. Great lesson of compromise!

Judgers like things to be organized. Judgers like to be on time, settled, planned, and decisive. They like to control their lives and—let's get really honest—they like to control other people's lives, too, because if you're not in line with a J's life, you're kind of messing it up. Judgers have a calendar and agenda and use them religiously. They like to create lists (and most importantly, they like to check things off their list). If you invite a Judger to a last-minute get together, chances are they're already booked or they might not want to come because it's so unexpected.

Perceiving people are flexible and spontaneous. They go with the flow and let life happen. Perceiving people are undaunted by surprise and enjoy the opportunity to do something flying by the seat of their pants. They don't tend to make plans too far in advance because they don't know if they'll be available. If something else that interests them more than what you have planned comes along, they might just opt to do something else.

Here are some words to describe Judging and Perceiving:

Judging	Perceiving
Organized	Pending
Settled	Flexible
Planned	Spontaneous
Decisive	Tentative
Controlled life	Let life happen
Set goals	Undaunted by surprise

Confusing J and P with S and N

There is very often confusion with the second (Sensing and Intuition) and the last (Judging and Perceiving) dichotomies. While I am typing someone in a workshop, corporate retreat, or one-on-one, there is sometimes confusion about how Sensing and Intuition correlate to Judging and Perceiving. Intuitive Types often think they must be a Judger because they are always thinking about the future, but nothing could be further from the truth. You can be an Intuitive Type and also a Perceiver; they are completely separate. Sensing and Intuition has to do with how we take in information, and the Judging and Perceiving dichotomy has to do with how we like to be organized in this world and how we like our world organized. You can still take in information via your intuition and always be thinking about what is next, but also be less structured and spontaneous, flitting from one thing to the next, like most NPs.

I hope you can start to see how each pairing plays a very special role in and of itself. In the next couple of sections, we are going to start pairing the dichotomies together to really have some fun and see them in a whole new way that will give you even deeper understanding.

Work *and* Play vs. Work *then* Play

Judgers like to work *then* play, meaning, they don't like to mix things; while Perceivers like to work *and* play, and can do both at the same time.

Imagine yourself at the office and a meeting is about to start. Before the meeting begins, Judgers and Perceivers are likely to be small talking. Even as the meeting starts there may be a little personal catching up going on, but at some point the Js will want the small talk to stop and the meeting to begin while Ps would prefer to continue with the fun, personal talk through the meeting. Ps can mix business and pleasure, while Js prefer them to be separate.

I was recently doing a keynote speech for a wonderful organization and the co-founders are two women, one an ENFP and the other an ISTJ. Late one evening we were doing a dry run of the next day, and the ISTJ CEO and I were sitting next to each other, wanting more than anything to get this over with quickly so we could go to bed and move on. The ENFP CEO was in rare "P" form that evening, having a blast working and playing at the same time, telling stories, and getting off topic nearly every chance she got. It was a perfect example of how Ps and Js prefer to work. The J CEO and I just wanted to get it done and the P CEO wanted to have some fun while we were working. It was a hilarious moment on stage the next day when I told that story to 800+ of their employees. They all loved it!

I told you this was funny! Can you see yourself and others more clearly in this dichotomy now?

How will you take this information and use it in your life, your relationships, and your business?

Don't Worry About It; We'll Figure It Out

"Don't worry about it; we'll figure it out." Ugh, don't *ever* say this to a J! While Ps like to go with the flow, figure things out as they go and assume everything will work out (and that is a great mentality to have), this stresses Js out and causes them anxiety.

I have worked with countless parents and their children over the years on this. P parents with J kids need to be aware that their "go with the flow" attitude does not work for their J kids that need to have a plan, need to have structure, and need to know what is going on. Children (and adults, for that matter) can show signs of anxiety and often think they need to be put on medication, but sometimes these J kids just need some structure in their lives.

I often think about the first day of school when it comes to this dichotomy. As a strong J, I used to worry for weeks about the first day of school. I would have nightmares about not knowing how to get to my classes or forgetting where my locker was. My mom would take me to school as soon as I received my schedule. We would walk the halls so I could map out where everything was and where I needed to be. Do this for your J kids—they need it. Often parents assume their children are just being difficult, but J kids really just need to know what is going on so they can relax and enjoy the rest of their summer or their day. This example really goes for anything—a typical Saturday, a vacation, and especially in your business. In order for a J to relax and be back in the present moment, they need to know the plan.

Js and Ps as Parents

This dichotomy/pairing can be challenging for parents.

Innate J moms or dads who typically like structure learn very quickly that they have to learn to go with the flow now that they are parents.

And innate P moms or dads who typically like to go with the flow learn very quickly that they have to learn to keep some sort of schedule or things fall through the cracks.

We all have things in our lives we simply have to do. Learning who you are innately is important so when you have to do the things you don't really like to do, you can understand it stretches you in ways that are going to cause you stress and you won't be at your best.

A parent who is a P may have to keep some sort of schedule, but they are at their best when they are simply playing and being spontaneous with their kids. And a J parent has to learn to go with the flow at times, but they are at their best when they can keep a clear schedule and keep on track.

I want you to choose all of these dichotomies based on who you are. Not you as a parent, as an employee, as a son, daughter, brother, or sister. But *you*, innately. Can you promise to do that?

Doing vs. Being

Ok, this is important. Judgers are "doers" innately and Perceivers are "be-ers" innately. However, as you are about to find out, this is the only dichotomy in which we don't get to say we suck at it so we won't waste our time on it. Js need to learn how to "be" and Ps need to learn how to "do."

To best explain this, I will tell you about two of my favorite clients, Lisa and Pia. Please note, their types are only one letter off. Lisa is an ENFP and Pia is an ENFJ.

Lisa is spontaneous, loves what she does and had no business plan whatsoever. She was running her business five minutes in front of her face and had no idea how to capitalize on the fact that she is a highly sought after, excellent stylist. She was a true NP and fought me for close to a year about "doing" since she was so good at "being," but she finally realized that was getting her nowhere in her business. She decided she wanted a successful business (and marriage, in fact) and decided it was time to buckle down and get serious about "doing." She, her business, and her marriage are almost unrecognizable today because of some hard work. She is organized (with some help). She is diligent about her work with me. Her marriage is the best it has ever been in 30 years. She is open and transparent. She is finally seeing the profit her work deserves because she quit making excuses for her P and decided to start learning how to "J out," as she calls it.

Now, it's not to say that this doesn't exhaust her—she needs some unstructured time to just be and to be silly, but she is now living both J and P. And because of the systems, structure, and singular focus I taught her, she gets to transform so many more lives.

Conversely, Pia is an ENFJ and has no problem doing; her problem is being. Pia is organized, runs a hugely successful brand/web design company, she is very detailed and quite controlling. Pia is also my web designer and has become a good friend. I went to Cabo last year and ran into her and her family there and she seemed so anxious. I asked her about it when we got home and she said it was because she couldn't just be, she needed to have a plan every minute of every day. Pia doesn't need me much as her business coach, but she really needs me as her life and relationship coach to help her just be. Pia is working on compartmentalizing her life so she can give 100% to her work when she is working and give 100% to her amazing family when she is with them.

It has been one of my greatest pleasures in life watching these two women embrace their personality type, learn from it, and make the necessary changes to do what they need to do to have a wonderful, well-rounded, successful life.

Judging World

While the Judging/Perceiving split is almost 50/50, we live in a world today where being driven, over-planned, and organized is rewarded. We see it everywhere from parents and schools over-scheduling activities and homework for children to Corporate America's endless meetings.

We live in a cell phone, "everything at your fingertips" generation, and this can be exhausting and overwhelming for everyone (but especially P types). They are wired to need no plans, no structure, to let life happen; and they get very little of that in today's overscheduled life. I see so many men and women in my practice who are at their wits' end trying to juggle the demands of life: working, raising children, taking vacations. They are burned out!

Since Js can handle the structure of today's world a bit better than Ps, Ps might need a break more often, possibly a day every week when they can do whatever strikes them in the moment. It isn't being lazy or irresponsible; it is simply who they are. Again, no judgment, remember?

I do this work because I want more acceptance for who we are innately so we can quit pathologizing each other. How much easier would your life be if you were allowed to be who you are innately more of the time? How much better would your relationships be if you loved your partner for who they are and quit trying to make them be who you want them to be? Learn this stuff. It will change your life and your relationships, I promise.

What others have to say...

Judgers About Perceivers

When Judgers were asked how they experienced Perceivers, they said they saw Perceivers as being:

- Flakey
- Unorganized
- Late
- Lazy
- Irritating

- Fun
- Spontaneous
- Enviable
- Go with the flow

Perceivers About Judgers

On the other hand, when I asked Perceivers how they see Judgers, they said they see Judgers as being:

- Rigid
- Controlling
- Uptight
- Annoying
- Organized

- Enviable
- Scheduled
- Need to be able to let go

"What I want you to know about me..."

Judgers

During that same exercise in my workshops, I also asked Judgers what they want Perceiver Types to know about them. Judgers want you to know:

- They are fun
- They need to know the plan in order to relax
- Don't ever say to them "don't worry about it, we will figure it out"—it stresses them out more
- They need a plan
- Your "no plan" attitude stresses them out
- Help by keeping somewhat of a weekly planner as a team or a family
- When you are late, they find it rude and disrespectful

Perceivers

- Your plans stress them out
- They need to have a day a week to just be, with no plans
- They aren't flakey; it is just the way they like to be

This Dude and Me

Since I have been single the last 4 years, I have dated a few "dudes" as I like to call them. I don't have many Ps in my life and when I started dating this one P dude a few years ago, my eyes were open to a whole new level of our differences.

One of the funniest differences is that I grocery shop once a week on Sundays after church. As a strong J, I clearly know my schedule for the week so I can plan what I need. It is also a huge time saver during the week that also allows me to eat healthy without wasting time going to the grocery store every day or having to stop and grab something unhealthy. Boring right? I get it.

This P dude didn't know what he was doing in an hour—let alone all week—so every single night he would either stop at the grocery store or stop to pick something up, and all my "super J" brain could think is "what a complete waste of time." I know, so judgy, but if you are a J you are totally thinking the same thing, aren't you?

Remember, there is no right and wrong way of being; we are just different and we can let those differences irritate us or we can use them to help "be" more or "do" more.

Anna

Anna is a Perceiving Type whom I have worked with for many years. She is an INFP, extremely sensitive, incredibly loving, very tuned into energy, and hates being a P. She gets so mad at herself for being a "go with the flow" person when she is surrounded by J energy. I have been encouraging her to find her tribe so that she feels at home and can start to embrace her awesome INFP self. She had been networking her business with driven, entrepreneurial women and feeling terrible about herself. She finally found a group of Reiki practitioners that share her "go with the flow" energy, and she is now finding her home. While she still needs to practice "doing" in her business, guilt-tripping herself all day isn't productive or helpful either. She is working on finding a balance between the two, just as we all are.

Which One Are You?

Judging or Perceiving?

I hope I have given you as much detail as you need to confidently choose which one you have a preference for, and to what degree (1—30). So take a moment and choose which one best describes you. Where do you think you fit on the Judging and Perceiving scale? Are you strongly Judging? Are you strongly Perceiving? Or are you somewhere in between? Indicate on the scale where you think you are.

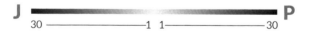

CHAPTER 6

Marginalized Types

"Your weirdness is likely your greatest asset"

—JIM ROHN

Before we end this section, it is important to remind you of the Types that often feel marginalized. They frequently describe feeling like they are on the outside looking in, misunderstood, or left out . If you have felt that way, you are likely one of these Types. As a business owner with a team of your own, it's important for you to bring out the best of your team in order to get their best performance. Expecting your team to do stuff they suck at and work outside of their Type is like pushing a boulder up a hill. So type your team, hire a consultant like me to come in and help everyone understand themselves, and let people do what they are good at. I guarantee it will be worth it! You will have happier, more engaged employees, and therefore have a better working environment and make more money! Doesn't that sound amazing??

Quick reminder of the marginalized types:

Introverts (I)—We live in an Extroverted world, so oftentimes Introverts find themselves trying hard to fit in by being an Extrovert or doing extroverted activities.

Intuitive (N)—With only 25% of the population as N Types, our world has been designed for Sensing Types. School, standardized tests, 9-5 corporate jobs, two weeks of vacation, and Monday through Friday work schedules are designed to fit Sensors' way of being. Intuitive Types have a very hard time fitting into that.

Feeling men (F)—Roughly 25% of men.

Thinking women (T)—Roughly 25% of women.

Perceivers (P)—We live in a world that rewards structure. Ps prefer to live spontaneously, which can often be met with judgment from our world designed on a time schedule.

INTP women—They often feel the most marginalized because we live in a Judging, planned world of Extroverted, Sensing, Feeling women.

INFP men—They feel similar for the same reasons as the women above because we live in a Judging, planned world of Extroverted, Sensing, Thinking men.

Are you in any of these categories? Or do you know anyone who fits in these categories? Stop judging them and start accepting them for their differences. It doesn't mean there is something wrong with them, or you, or any of us. We are who we are, so let's start embracing our differences instead of letting them tear us apart.

CHAPTER 7

Whole Letter Type

"The need to be normal is the predominant anxiety disorder in modern life."

—THOMAS MOORE

Before we can move on to the heart of this book, you must be confident with your preferences covered in the last section:

Extroversion / Introversion
Sensing / Intuition
Thinking / Feeling
Judging / Perceiving

The four dichotomies are extremely important to understand and invaluable in and of themselves. However, we are about to dig much deeper into *you*: your energy, how people see you, your best self, how you react during stress, and the things you need to avoid in your life, relationships, and work.

At this point, there will be a few of you that are still struggling with determining your type. In my experience, there are always a few people that have a hard time determining their preference between one or more of the pairings. If that is where you are, this section will help you get clear on your type. The Type Table below shows the 16 different Myers-Briggs Types. You have a preference for one of them, again, with varying degrees of strength. If you are struggling between whether you have a preference for Introversion or Extroversion, but you are clear about the last three letters, then read the two descriptions of the two different whole types and one will resonate much more with you. For example, if you are clear on your NFP but not sure about whether you have a preference for Introversion and Extroversion, then read both ENFP and INFP and one will be a much better fit. You will see there is a big difference between an ENFP and an INFP. One letter makes a huge difference throughout the rest of the book, so it is important to be clear about your type before moving on.

Type Table

ISTJ	ISFJ	INFJ	INTJ
1. Sensing	1. Sensing	1. Intuition	1. Intuition
2. Thinking	2. Feeling	2. Feeling	2. Thinking
3. Feeling	3. Thinking	3. Thinking	3. Feeling
4. Intuition	4. Intuition	4. Sensing	4. Sensing
ISTP	**ISFP**	**INFP**	**INTP**
1. Thinking	1. Feeling	1. Feeling	1. Thinking
2. Sensing	2. Sensing	2. Intuition	2. Intuition
3. Intuition	3. Intuition	3. Sensing	3. Sensing
4. Feeling	4. Thinking	4. Thinking	4. Feeling
ESTP	**ESFP**	**ENFP**	**ENTP**
1. Sensing	1. Sensing	1. Intuition	1. Intuition
2. Thinking	2. Feeling	2. Feeling	2. Thinking
3. Feeling	3. Thinking	3. Thinking	3. Feeling
4. Intuition	4. Intuition	4. Sensing	4. Sensing
ESTJ	**ESFJ**	**ENFJ**	**ENTJ**
1. Thinking	1. Feeling	1. Feeling	1. Thinking
2. Sensing	2. Sensing	2. Intuition	2. Intuition
3. Intuition	3. Intuition	3. Sensing	3. Sensing
4. Feeling	4. Thinking	4. Thinking	4. Feeling

Now that you've successfully completed the first section, take a moment and put together those four letters. Fill in your whole letter type here: _____.

Introverted Types:

- ISTJ - The Duty Filler
- ISFJ - The Nurturer
- INFJ - The Protector
- INTJ - The Scientist
- ISTP - The Mechanic
- ISFP - The Artist
- INFP - The Idealist
- INTP - The Thinker

Extroverted Types:

- ESTP - The Doer
- ESFP - The Performer
- ENFP - The Inspirer
- ENTP - The Visionary
- ESTJ - The Guardian
- ESFJ - The Caregiver
- ENFJ - The Giver
- ENTJ - The Executive

Due to copyright laws, I cannot provide you the full Myers-Briggs descriptions (which are the best and I did not write). You can find them on my website at **www.jessicabutts.com** under the "My Book" tab. I encourage you to go there now and read about your whole full letter type. You'll discover positive and negative traits about your type. Have an open mind. You will probably think something like, "This is so me!" Most people feel extremely validated at this point because they have the experience of reading about themselves.

The descriptions by Myers-Briggs are written for people with clear to strong preferences (10–30), so if you have a slight preference (1–9), some of what you read might not quite fit. That is OK. If your personality dichotomy is slight rather than strong, try switching the letter you feel doesn't describe you well and then find your full type description to see if that type sounds more like you. If something about a specific type doesn't quite ring true for you, look at the pairs again and maybe switch out one of the letters to see if that makes more sense to you. For example, if you are an ENFP but only slight on the P, also read ENFJ and see which one resonates with you more.

You can find a free, fun, and accurate one on my website.

Excellent work so far! I know I've said it before, but this is really just the beginning. Now we are about to have some real fun. I have been using type for over 20 years, and my Live Your Life from the Front Seat™ method (as well as my unique version of archetypes) will help you see yourself and others in your life so much more clearly. It will give you new language to bring into your life, relationships, and work to help you start living an authentic, kick-ass life (and an incredibly successful business).

CHAPTER 8

Group/Team Type

If you are like most people, you have undoubtedly been typing your coworkers and team as we have been going on this journey of exploring your type. Now that you have your whole letter type, and likely have typed a few others in your life, we can talk about group and/or team Type.

I have talked about the marginalized Types and how tough it can be as the one feeling left out. Well, the same goes for groups or teams. The best way I can explain this is to show you a couple of examples. The first is a small company of six where I recently did a workshop.

Here are the employees' types: ENFP ENFP INFP ESTP ISFP ENFJ

Group Type = ENFP

To determine this group's Type, you simply add up the sum of the letters.

> 4 Extroverts vs. 2 Introverts = Extrovert (E)
> 2 Sensors vs. 4 Intuitive = Intuitive (N)
> 1 Thinker vs. 5 Feelers = Feeler (F)
> 1 Judger vs. 5 Perceivers = Perceiver (P)

This group's type is an ENFP because the majority of the employees are Extroverted, Intuitive, Feeling, and Perceiving; therefore, the group dynamic is mostly ENFP.

Once the group could see it laid out like this, the light bulbs started going off. The manager, the ENFJ (and the only J in the group) realized *why* he had been so frustrated with everyone. He felt as if he was the only one who cared about the small company because he was the only one who came to work on time each day, set and followed all the rules, and couldn't understand their laid-back attitudes. The rest of the group explained it wasn't as if they didn't care, they just had a different way of being, a more laid-back approach to life and business. They like to work and play at the same time.

The other marginalized person in the organization was a woman and the only Thinker in the group. She always felt as if she didn't want to get involved with the "touchy feely" stuff with customers, clients, or the other staff. Once she saw why, she felt as if she could finally verbalize it to the group without judgment. There wasn't anything wrong with her; she was just the only Thinking Type in the group.

My second example is another small company of four I worked with a few years ago. Their Types are as follows:

CEO—ENTP
President—ENTP
Office manager—ISFJ
Assistant—ESTP
Group Type = ES/NTP

Their group type is Extroverted, split between Sensing and Intuition, Thinker and Perceiver. As you can imagine, the office manager (ISFJ) felt marginalized, weird, and left out a lot of the time in the team based on the group Type dynamic. Once the team learned all their types and could see their Types clearly, they realized they needed to allow their office manager to be alone when she needed to be, without judgment. They also realized she needed a little emotional support to fulfill her Feeling Type and that they needed to provide more structure for her J-ness.

Understanding group Type can lead to so much more awareness and understanding of each other. I hope this is something you will consider doing with every group in your life so you can better understand the dynamic of the group and where you land in it.

CHAPTER 9

Archetypical View

There are a number of ways to break down Type. You are already familiar with dichotomies and whole letter Type.

We started with the individual dichotomies by Myers-Briggs that tell us so much about ourselves and our relationships.

As you saw, the whole letter Type can be a roadmap filled with words and concepts to help us better understand ourselves and tell others how to treat us.

Another fun way to look at Type is by an archetypal view, which can help us get unstuck if we're struggling with a couple of letters in our whole letter type.

I want to provide usable, funny, accurate language to use in our workplace to understand the four parts of our innateness

NP—Squirrel
NJ—Entrepreneurs
SP—Just Do It
SJ—The Police

I want to make this work accessible and understandable—something you can talk to your team about, use at the office, with your partner, friends, and family. Over the years, I have discovered my own version of archetypes which are the second and last letter of your type. I believe you will find it not only accurate, but also easy to relate to and understand.

I hope each of these different ways of looking at Type gives you a language and/or framework you can use. We each have these archetypes in our lives, and seeing them from this quirky vantage will, I hope, give you a unique perspective into how we all operate and see the world differently. We are all innately born with our Type, so understanding ourselves better can deeply enhance our relationships with ourselves and others.

It is part of my unique brilliance to help people understand complex things in a way that's easy to digest. I hope these archetypes do just that for you.

NP—Intuitive Perceiving Types
ENFP, INFP, EN TP, IN TP Squirrel

Remember in that movie *UP*, when the dog was paying attention to his owner one moment, but as soon as a squirrel came nearby, he completely lost his concentration and focus and was immediately distracted? NP Types, that's you.

Intuitive Perceiving Types are very easily distracted by bright and shiny objects. They have a lot of ideas (Intuition), but get easily distracted by the next greatest thing and have a tendency not to follow through (Perceiving).

NPs are the gypsies of the world. They may never seem settled and actually prefer it that way. They are constantly on to the next greatest thing or adventure. They want new, rich, and unique experiences.

As I was working on this book, I did some research on the different archetypes. I interviewed people I know and asked them to share words they felt described themselves well.

NPs described themselves as:

- Creative
- Warm
- Easygoing
- Curious
- Loyal
- Adaptable
- Caring
- Insightful

NPs make great idea generators and coaches. Their minds are alive all the time with ideas and possibilities. They are excellent at thinking outside the box and creating new and interesting content. Think of them as big picture be-ers. They are also the most "woo woo" of all the archetypes, typically into yoga, alternative healing and ways of being. They do, however, get bored very easily and do not like to have to finish a project. They can benefit from having an S or J or SJ on the team to help them with the details. NP Squirrels and SJ Police drive each other crazy, but can make an excellent team in getting things done. The NP Squirrel has excellent ideas and the SJ police can help execute those ideas. Remember to always be aware of our irritating behaviors and be thankful to our opposite Types. They're there to help us! NPs need to be aware that they are hard to pin down, hard to schedule, and hard to keep on time, and yes, it irritates people, but we want to love you anyway so just be aware of it.

NJ—Intuitive Judging Types
ENFJ, INFJ, INTJ, ENTJ Entrepreneur

NJs are the entrepreneurs of the world. They have a lot of ideas just like the NPs, but are decisive decision makers, which means they get a lot of stuff done. Unfortunately, NJs don't work very well with change, as they like things systematic, organized, and structured. When things get in their way, it causes them to feel flustered. NJs are not great at the details, but can still get things done.

NJs are excellent "getter done-ers." They have big ideas and usually run with them before they have given any

NJs described themselves as:

- Persistent
- Enthusiastic
- Loyal
- Insightful
- Planful
- Curious
- Compassionate
- Encouraging
- Inquisitive

thought to what the facts or data say about their idea, and they have *no* interest in market research. They are great at start-ups, ideas, project management, and helping others see possibilities. They are idea generators. They are idea doers. They can also be quite controlling, rigid, and want things done their way. I am an NJ and my NJ clients excite me but also exhaust me. They keep me on my toes and typically have a lot of masculine/bossy energy.

SP—Sensing Perceiving Types
ESFP, ISFP, ESTP, ISTP Just Do It

The Sensing Perceiving (SP) Types are all about experiencing the world and everything in it. The Sensing (S) Type is about the here and now and taking in information via their five senses, while the Perceiving (P) Type wants to be spontaneous and just go with it. This combination equals a "Just do it" mentality. Whether they're Introverted or Extroverted, they are fun, active, and engaged people. They do this in many ways: through music, art, climbing rocks, jumping off cliffs—it doesn't matter. They just need to be experiencing something.

SPs are the ultimate in, "Don't worry about it; we will figure it out!" They don't typically have a plan outside of right now and are go with the flow kinds of people who like to live in the moment. They are great with details, data, and facts as long as

SPs described themselves as:
- Playful
- Present
- Empathetic
- Go along with others
- Open
- Listener
- Hearing
- Unscripted
- Fly by the seat of their pants
- Whatever works
- Others first
- Unplanned
- Organized but flexible
- Relaxed

they can play a little with it. I have found SPs to be very loyal employees because they don't usually have a long-term plan for their careers, and as long as they like what they are doing, you are likely to have a happy and loyal member of your team. However, they do like some play in their work, so keep that in mind when scheduling meetings and work functions. They are great 9-5 people, but enjoy some play and occasional happy hour after work to just "be."

SJ—Sensing Judging Types
ESFJ, ISFJ, ESTJ, ISTJ The Police

Sensing Judging (SJ) Types are the Police. They are responsible, value-driven, hard-working, reliable, but sometimes a little rigid. They like structure, schedules, and routine. If anyone needs something done, they know they can count on an SJ to do it. Sensing allows them to be practical and in the moment, while Judging keeps them organized and planned.

SJs are the ultimate rule-follower and excellent employees—as long as they are treated with respect! SJs value hard work, integrity, and respect, and when that is lost it is hard to keep their values-driven personality happy. Facts, data, details, organization, and fairness drive the SJs, and if they are treated fairly you have an excellent, loyal, and hard-working employee! SJs are hard-working, driven people whether they are the boss or the employee, but they

SJs described themselves as:
- Disciplined
- Organized
- Trustworthy
- Dependable
- Realistic
- Thoughtful
- Orderly
- Careful
- Innovative
- Multitasker
- Impulsive
- Optimistic
- Leader
- Driven
- Creative

need to be respected for their integrity and hard work.

I believe you must have some opposites on your team to help you with the areas that you suck at. Quit trying to do everything and find people who want to help you and are innately good at the things you aren't. I know it is tough at first, but you will very quickly realize how much more effective you can be and how it will pay for itself in the extra revenue you will easily make doing only your Front Seat activities in your business.

I love dissecting and playing with the work by Myers-Briggs and creating an uncommon way of looking at it. My intention and hope is that you can see yourself in a new light and use these fun ways to put this amazing tool to work in your business.

We are now going to embark on the ultimate creation of my Intuitive brain, and that is how to Live Your Life from the Front Seat. Buckle up, because we are going to jump into the car of your personality to see exactly how it runs when you are at your best, when you're doing the things you suck at, and where you go when you are spending too much time doing those things.

SECTION 2

Roadmap to Your Front Seat Life

Live Your Life from

the Front Seat™

CHAPTER 10

Live Your Life from the Front Seat

*"We will never be great at the things
we have to try to be good at."*

—MARCUS BUCKINGHAM

We have been going over Myers-Briggs work thus far, but I am now going to introduce you to my take on this work. I call it Live Your Life from the Front Seat™. I have noticed a problem over the 20+ years I have been working with Type—people can't remember all the letters; they always struggle with what letters they are, in what order they go, and what they even mean. Therefore, they don't use it and that is such a shame because, as I hope you are starting to see, there is great power in understanding your innateness. Living our lives and running our businesses based on how we were created is an amazing, congruent feeling, and one that I want for all of you.

If you are currently doing a pretty good job of living your life from the Front Seat, then this will further enhance the correct path you are on. But, if you are like most people and living your life from the Back Seat, this section might be a little painful. There may even be some tears at this point, because people realize they have been spending most of their time and energy from the Back Seat, which you are about to learn is a drain of our energy big time. This is especially true in business since so many of us, me included, choose the wrong careers for our innate personality Types and then can't seem to figure out why we hate it so much. How many of you choose a major in college or a career because you either had to, your parents chose it for you, or you simply fell into it? Or you are running your business and trying to do everything?

I hope at this point you realize there are things you are innately good at and things you suck at. If you are still trying to do all things in your business, you have likely been unsuccessful or hit a major wall or both. My experience is that close to 100% of people, again me included, have no idea who they are when asked to make this choice in their early 20s! We then spend 10 to 20 years doing something we innately suck at and we have no energy, we are depressed, we hate getting up in the morning, we live for the weekend, we probably drink too much on those weekends to numb the pain of the job we hate, etc. It is a vicious cycle I have seen literally thousands of times.

If you are one of those people, I get it; I was there too. The good news is you can do something about it. I am not saying it is going to be easy, but you can redesign your life and your work around what you are actually good at and love doing. How does that sound? Hang in there; we are just getting to the really good stuff.

So now we are going to get even deeper and more specific about your Type and your unique brilliance. The MBTI breaks our Type down into four areas that most people find a little difficult to understand.

- Dominant
- Auxillary
- Tertiary
- Inferior

I have developed what I hope is a much easier way to understand these four important areas of our personality, including how and when they show up. We are going to talk a lot about the passengers in your car for the remainder of this book, and my hope is that this will become a new part of your language. I am about to give you a specific roadmap to exactly where you should be spending your energy, what your unique brilliance is in this world, areas you must avoid, and where you go in times of deep stress. You ready? Here we go…

Your Car

Please imagine a car with four seats, preferably your car, if yours has four seats. Those four seats represent different parts of your personality; they are all part of you. You have a Driver and a Copilot, which represent the Front Seats. You have two passengers in the Back Seat that I have named the Drunk Uncle and the Baby in the Back Seat.

Driver
Copilot
Drunk Uncle in the Back Seat
Baby in the Back Seat

    Now, I want you to imagine yourself in your car as all four passengers. Close your eyes for just a moment after reading this, and really get a mental picture of yourself in your car. Visualize yourself as the driver, then as the copilot, an uncle passed out in the back seat, and as a baby in a car seat in the back seat. Now, close your eyes and really see this image of these parts of your personality in your car. This should be an interesting image to see yourself as multiple people in the same car, but this is what your personality Type is like. All these different people are different aspects of your personality.

    Now take your four-letter Type from Chapter 7 and match it to the corresponding passengers in your car. Please write your words for each passenger (Driver, Copilot, Drunk Uncle and Baby) into the diagram on Page 81. I also outline this on the free assessment on my website at www.jessicabutts.com. If you have any confusion at all you can go take that assessment now.

I want you to have this visual as we go into the next section. I will outline every car, including yours, but it is important to write this in now so you have it when we cover your Front Seat and Back Seat in detail.

ISTJ - The Duty Filler
Driver: Introverted Sensing
Copilot: Extroverted Thinking
Drunk Uncle in the Back Seat: Introverted Feeling
Baby in the Back Seat: Extroverted Intuition

ISFJ - The Nurturer
Driver: Introverted Sensing
Copilot: Extroverted Feeling
Drunk Uncle in the Back Seat: Introverted Thinking
Baby in the Back Seat: Extroverted Intuition

INFJ - The Protector
Driver: Introverted Intuition
Copilot: Extroverted Feeling
Drunk Uncle in the Back Seat: Introverted Thinking
Baby in the Back Seat: Extroverted Sensing

INTJ - The Scientist
Driver: Introverted Intuition
Copilot: Extroverted Thinking
Drunk Uncle in the Back Seat: Introverted Feeling
Baby in the Back Seat: Extroverted Sensing

ISTP - The Mechanic
Driver: Introverted Thinking
Copilot: Extroverted Sensing
Drunk Uncle in the Back Seat: Introverted Intuition
Baby in the Back Seat: Extroverted Feeling

ISFP - The Artist
Driver: Introverted Feeling
Copilot: Extroverted Sensing
Drunk Uncle in the Back Seat: Introverted Intuition
Baby in the Back Seat: Extroverted Thinking

INFP - The Idealist
Driver: Introverted Feeling
Copilot: Extroverted Intuition
Drunk Uncle in the Back Seat: Introverted Sensing
Baby in the Back Seat: Extroverted Thinking

INTP - The Thinker
Driver: Introverted Thinking
Copilot: Extroverted Intuition
Drunk Uncle in the Back Seat: Introverted Sensing
Baby in the Back Seat: Extroverted Feeling

ESTP - The Doer
Driver: Extroverted Sensing
Copilot: Introverted Thinking
Drunk Uncle in the Back Seat: Extroverted Feeling
Baby in the Back Seat: Introverted Intuition

ESFP - The Performer
Driver: Extroverted Sensing
Copilot: Introverted Feeling
Drunk Uncle in the Back Seat: Extroverted Thinking
Baby in the Back Seat: Introverted Intuition

ENFP - The Inspirer
Driver: Extroverted Intuition
Copilot: Introverted Feeling
Drunk Uncle in the Back Seat: Extroverted Thinking
Baby in the Back Seat: Introverted Sensing

ENTP - The Visionary
Driver: Extroverted Intuition
Copilot: Introverted Thinking
Drunk Uncle in the Back Seat: Extroverted Feeling
Baby in the Back Seat: Introverted Sensing

ESTJ - The Guardian
Driver: Extroverted Thinking
Copilot: Introverted Sensing
Drunk Uncle in the Back Seat: Extroverted Intuition
Baby in the Back Seat: Introverted Feeling

ESFJ - The Caregiver
Driver: Extroverted Feeling
Copilot: Introverted Sensing
Drunk Uncle in the Back Seat: Extroverted Intuition
Baby in the Back Seat: Introverted Thinking

ENFJ - The Giver
Driver: Extroverted Feeling
Copilot: Introverted Intuition
Drunk Uncle in the Back Seat: Extroverted Sensing
Baby in the Back Seat: Introverted Thinking

ENTJ - The Executive
Driver: Extroverted Thinking
Copilot: Introverted Intuition
Drunk Uncle in the Back Seat: Extroverted Sensing
Baby in the Back Seat: Introverted Feeling

Full Car

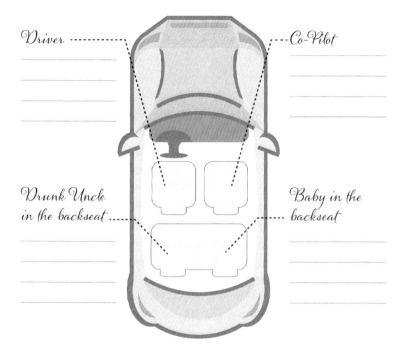

Now that you have your car filled out, let's get specific about each of the passengers in your car and what they represent in your life, and more specifically your business, so you can start doing what you are innately good at. This will attract your ideal clients and make you more money (while making you much happier and able to quit doing stuff you suck at)!

Remember the visual of the passengers in your car taking a cross country trip—this is who I am about to describe. If you need further visual help, there are some videos on my website (www.jessicabutts.com) and YouTube channel you can watch to help you get clear.

CHAPTER 11

Your Front Seat

"Being your true self is the most effective formula for success there is."

—DANIELLE LAPORTE

One thing has happened universally to everyone reading this book and everyone on earth—we have all been born. We are all born into this world with our unique and special personality Type for a reason. We are all born with our personality Types and, as I have said before, our Type does not change; our life circumstances change.

Each of the four dichotomies and our whole letter Type indicate career preferences. This is not absolute, and the strength of our preference has a large impact on this. However, this is generally true for most people most of the time.

> **Extroverts** prefer working with others and giving to others since they give their best self to others.
>
> **Introverts** prefer to work alone as they give their best selves to themselves. They get drained by being with others too much.
>
> **Intuitives** need to think outside the box and prefer to make their own schedule, and they must have creativity and variety in their work.

Sensors prefer having a schedule and routine, and they work better knowing what to expect.

Thinkers prefer to do work where they can use logic and reasoning and not have to deal with emotions (others or their own).

Feelers prefer to deal with people, relationships, and deep meaning.

Judgers need to have a plan and be in control. Unscheduled meetings, no deadlines, and tardiness make Judgers crazy.

Perceivers need to have variety and prefer a much more flexible work schedule. They prefer to work on their own schedule.

The fact is, it is easier and takes less energy to be who we were designed to be—it just is!

It takes effort to be in our Back Seats and do things we suck at. It drains us, makes us depressed, cranky, and as you will learn, makes our Baby in the Back Seat wake up and she/he is not so pleasant.

There was a philosophy back in the 80s that we should all be balanced and work on the things we aren't good at. I call bullshit on that! Don't do stuff you suck at. Why waste your energy?

We only have so much energy. Why not spend the majority of yours doing things you are great at? That is where you have your best energy—energy that attracts the right people into your life, your ideal clients, makes you more money, and makes you happier. Why would we not do that? Because society tells us differently. Don't listen to them!

Your Front Seat is where you want to be spending at least 80% of your time! I promise you, if you start spending that much time in your Front Seat, your life will change for the better. You will:

- Show up authentically
- Have better energy
- Do better work
- Sleep better
- Have deeper connections with people
- Make more money
- Be happier
- Likely lose weight
- Feel better
- Feel a sense of freedom
- Attract the right people/clients/friends into your life

Honestly, shame on us for not doing this! If we are wasting our time in our Back Seats we are doing such a disservice to ourselves, our friends, our jobs, our spouses, and our kids! Do you want to be giving your wonky energy to the people in your life? I certainly hope not! So, it is time to start Living Your Life from the Front Seat. I will show you exactly how, now that you know your four-letter Myers-Briggs Type. This next section is going to walk you through your Front Seat, your best self, and where you should be spending 80% of your time. And then we will talk about the dreaded Back Seat drivers and where you must stop spending your time. How? By acknowledging that you suck at this stuff, and then asking for help in these areas. Ready? Let's go.

Driver: *Your Best Self*

Go back to imagining yourself in your car. Let's start with you as the driver.

Your Driver is your best self and in charge of you. When you imagine the car, this is the person who knows where you are going, decides your path, how fast you are going, and is in control of the car. He/she is actually leading all the others in the car by being in charge. The Driver has his/her eyes on the road and can see where you are going. This is the person we want to find in you so we can cultivate it and bring it out the most.

When you are living in accordance with your Driver, the right people respond to you and are drawn to you. It is your healthiest and most authentic self—truly you at your best. It is your unique brilliance in the world. Your Driver (and Copilot, which make up your Front Seat) is you being authentic. And everyone feels better when they are living an authentic life. Everyone! It is also easy because it is *you*, how you were designed. When you are spending 80% of your time doing these things in your business, you are in your flow, in your groove, in the vortex, in your jam...whatever you want to call it. You are kickin' ass and taking names from your Front Seat. Your ideal clients will respond to you when you are coming from this place of authenticity.

If you're an Extrovert, you're giving your best self to the world. Let me say that again—if you are an Extrovert, you are giving your best self to the world. You are likely very similar in many areas of your life: at home, at work, with friends, and with clients. If you're not, you should be.

If you're an Introvert you're saving your best self for yourself. Most people don't know the best part of you because you save that for yourself or those very close to you. So what the world sees of you is your Copilot (your second-best self).

Remember the 'heart on your sleeve' analogy from Chapter 2.

Ok, now for the Introvert. Introverts wear their hearts on the inside of their sleeves. It is not visible to everyone. They must actually invite someone to get close to them physically and emotionally in order to see the heart on the inside of their sleeve, they choose to show it or not.

Copilot: *Your Second-Best Self*

Imagine yourself back in your car; your Copilot is an important part of your journey. This part of your personality is your wingman, your Copilot on the journey of life—and is your second-best self.

If you are an Extrovert, your Driver is an Extrovert, which means your Copilot must be an Introvert. If you are an Introvert, your Driver is an Introvert which means your Copilot must be an Extrovert. We can't have our two Front Seat drivers both be Introverted or Extroverted—they must balance each other out. If both Front Seat passengers were Extroverted, no one would ever want to be around you because you would never shut up, and if both were Introverted you would never leave the house. Since this is where we need to be spending 80% of our time, one must be given to the world and one must be saved for ourselves.

If you are an Introvert, you save your best self for yourself and give your Copilot self to the world. If you are an Extrovert, you give your Driver to the world and save your Copilot self for yourself. Same concept, different energy. Neither is better than the other, they are just different.

As an ENFJ, my Driver is an Extroverted Feeler. That means I give my best self to the world. My Copilot is an Introverted Intuitive. That means in my head I'm always generating ideas, always thinking about what's next. We work in harmony because this is my Front Seat. This is where I am my best. I come up with ideas. I have them in my head. I'm thinking about what's next and where I'm going. I'm visioning. I'm future thinking, but I'm also out there in the world giving myself, my *best* self, to the world.

Who are these two people in the Front Seat for you? How do they show up in your life? What do they represent? More importantly, are you using them correctly and to their full potential?

Unfortunately, many of us are not functioning from our Front Seat. We're working in jobs where we are doing things that we're not really that good at and which suck the energy out of us. We're in relationships where we feel we're being drained of energy and life. I know that this resonates with many people, so my goal is to get it to stop so you can start living your life and running your business from your Front Seat and avoid the dreaded Back Seat passengers we are about to discuss.

CHAPTER 12

Your Back Seat

"Don't do stuff you suck at."

—JESSICA BUTTS

Now onto the two dreaded Back Seat drivers in your car: the Drunk Uncle and the Baby in the Back Seat. Both show up when you are doing things that you simply should not be doing. You know your Drunk Uncle or Baby is in charge when you feel stressed out and at your wits' end. This is not a time you want a drunk person or a baby making any decisions about your life.

Both the Drunk Uncle and the Baby in the Back Seat have bad, wonky energy! You are not at your best when either one of these two Back Seat drivers is in charge! So let's spend a little time digging into these two very important, but yucky, people in your car.

Drunk Uncle in the Back Seat:
What You Should Not Be Doing

Imagine yourself back in your car. The first passenger in the Back Seat is your Drunk Uncle. Unfortunately, we all probably know someone like this in our family, or have been drunk ourselves. Drunks are a mess. They slur their words, they take much longer to do any task or make a decision, and it's likely that it won't be done well since it is being done while intoxicated. We are repelled by drunk people—they are annoying and we would rather not be around them. We would much prefer they simply pass out in the back seat and take a little drunken nap.

We all have things in our lives we suck at, and based on your personality, I will show you exactly what yours are. I want you to stop doing them, completely, if possible. If you have designed your life around your Back Seat, it may take a while for you to quit doing these completely at first. But as you work through this and I map out your car for you, you will start to see why doing these things does no good for anyone in your life, especially you.

Back Seat energy is a waste of your effort and your time. Imagine a drunk person running your life or your business! No, thank you! Whatever it is, let someone else do it for you. Remember, we can't be good at everything. Give yourself a break and stop trying, for goodness sake. Balance is so 80s and an outdated concept. Just do what you are good at. You will be happier, make more money, and your energy will be so much better, I promise you!

When we take jobs that suck our happiness or when we stay in relationships that don't make us feel strong, happy, and supported, it just makes sense that we feel completely drained of energy.

That is why I want you to start living your life from the Front Seat, not this wonky, drunk Back Seat energy. Ideally, I would like you to spend 0% of your time as your Drunk Uncle, but at the maximum 10%.

Who knows this energy? It is sad, exhausting, and it feels like you are constantly pushing a boulder up a hill. It takes *so* much energy to be doing things you innately suck at all day long. As a business coach, I see this every single day—entrepreneurs trying to do everything in their businesses. I know, I get that money is tight when you are starting a business and hiring someone feels out of reach. I have been there; I get it. So you have two choices: (1) you can risk doing those things in your business and hope it doesn't cause catastrophic results like huge mistakes, time suck, or (even worse) depression or quitting because you just can't handle it anymore, or (2) you can realize that this is the best investment you are going to make in your business and hire someone to help you do the stuff you suck at, likely at a fraction of the price of your hourly rate. Then you can spend your valuable time making money and doing what you are great at.

Here's a point of clarification. If you have a very strong preference, your Drunk Uncle activities are extremely intoxicated. If you have a slight preference, these activities are like you're simply buzzed. So, I want to give a warning to all of you who have a strong preference: you need to avoid your Drunk Uncle activities more than everyone else.

Here's the deal with your Drunk Uncle activities: When you do them it causes sadness, anxiety, stress, worry, doubt, and even depression. Yes, even depression. For real. So if you are spending a good amount of time doing these things, you can expect something really bad to happen—your Baby in the Back Seat wakes up and takes over, and that is *not* a good thing. Let's discuss that part of your personality now, as it is mostly caused by doing things you suck at all day, which are your Drunk Uncle activities.

Baby in the Back Seat:
You Under Stress

Your last personality Type is your inferior Type, which I call the Baby in the Back Seat. It seems funny, but it's actually quite serious. When you are stressed out, when your back is up against the wall, when someone has pushed you to your limit, when a job has you at our wits' end, and most importantly, when you are spending your time doing things you suck at in your business, your Baby in the Back Seat takes over and every other part of your personality shuts down.

Whoever your Driver is, your Baby is the exact opposite, and in an extremely negative context.

If your Driver is Introverted, your Baby in the Back Seat is Extroverted. If you're normally quiet and reserved, your Baby comes out screaming and yelling. It scares people because it's behaving exactly opposite of who you normally are. People will say, "Gosh, you're so different," and the reality is—you are. It is so important to not judge yourself about this, but just to be aware of how powerful an impact the Baby in the Back Seat has.

If your Driver is Extroverted, your Baby in Back Seat is Introverted. When you are stressed out or at your wits' end as an Extrovert, you retreat and hide from the world. Your normal outgoing self has to take a break from your normal Extroverted energy. Your friends may wonder where you went, why you aren't calling or posting on Facebook—it is likely because you don't want to leave the house or even your bed.

I know I don't want a drunk person or a baby running my life or my business. A drunk is a mess and makes mistakes, and a baby is immature and the opposite of my best self. These two parts of ourselves are extremely dangerous to our energy, our jobs, and our relationships. We need to learn how to keep them to a minimum.

Every time I am giving a talk and I get to the Baby in the Back Seat someone (or multiple people) in the audience begins to cry. That is always a sign that the person has been living their life from the Back Seat and they know how awful it feels to be functioning from this place. Consider these experiences: bad relationships, wrong jobs, doing too many Drunk Uncle activities, someone hurting you. All can keep you functioning in your Back Seat for days or, in many cases, years.

Our Reptilian Brain and the Baby in the Back Seat

Warning: I'm going to nerd out for a minute.

Our brain has many important parts, but the two parts I am going to discuss with you are our prefrontal cortex and our reptilian brain.

Our prefrontal cortex is there for reasoning; it is what sets us apart from all other animals. It allows us to make decisions, have reasoning, and be rational.

Our reptilian brain is that of a reptile, its primary function is to fight or to flee.

You can think of your Baby in the Back Seat as flipping your prefrontal cortex up and only using your reptilian brain. All our reasoning and rational thoughts have gone out the door. We are solely fighting or fleeing, and we are designed to do one or the other. We are in protection mode when our Baby in the Back Seat wakes up; she/he is keeping us safe from harm, but again, not in a good or rational way.

Extroverts flee; they run away, they hide. Their typical, normal, Driver self is out in the world giving their best selves. When they are stressed out, at their wits' end or spending too much time doing stuff they suck at in their businesses, their reasoning goes away and the reptilian brain wakes up to protect them. They do whatever is necessary to retreat.

Introverts fight; they yell, they scream, they pick fights. Their typical, normal, Driver self is more quiet and reserved, saving their best selves for themselves. When they are stressed out, at their wits' end or spending too much time doing stuff they suck at, their reasoning goes away and the reptilian brain wakes up to protect them. They do whatever is necessary to come out fighting.

I want you to take some time to write how your Baby in the Back Seat shows up for you. Can you identify areas in your business that when you do them too much your Baby in the Back Seat wakes up and you either fight or flee? Our Baby is going to show up; that is a fact! But we can also be aware of how and when our Baby shows up and do some things to get us back into the Front Seat.

Front Seat Activities

Again, it is perfectly okay to get into our Back Seats occasionally. It is going to happen. Instead of beating ourselves up about it, we can sit with it, and then learn some activities to pull ourselves out of that Back Seat and get us back into our kick-ass Front Seat.

Examples of Front Seat activities:

Extroverts:	Being with people
	Talking with a friend
	Dancing
Introverts:	Cooking alone
	Journaling
	Reading
	Deep conversation with a great friend
Intuitives:	Being creative
	White space to just imagine
Sensors:	Making a list
	Doing something with their hands or body
NP:	Starting a new, fun project
SP:	Being active with hands or body

NJ:	Creating something new
SJ:	Taking care of something
All Types:	Taking a walk in nature, either alone or with a friend (nature and water help ground us) Making and playing a Front Seat music playlist Reaching out for help (every type needs to know they are not alone)

What are your Front Seat activities? Make an exhaustive list here. This is incredibly important and we will use this again in the next section. It is equally important to know what puts us in the Back Seat as it is to know how to get ourselves back into our Front Seats. Let me be very clear here: If you are not running your business from your Front Seat, it is not going to be successful. Period. It may last for a while, but long term it is going to fail if you cannot identify your innate Front Seat goodness and your yucky Back Seat wonkiness.

I rarely do anything in my Back Seat. I have created a life for myself in which I rarely do any of my Drunk Uncle activities anymore (which, for me, are Sensing activities). I spend less time in my Back Seat than I used to now that I have designed a life around my type. But on the rare occasion when I am my Baby in the Back Seat, I don't do anything of importance. I rest and allow the feelings to be with me for as long as they need to. I process fully through journaling, walking, resting, napping, or talking to a friend. Then I pull myself out of the Back Seat, put my big girl panties back on, and get back into my Driver's seat by doing some Front Seat activities.

Here are examples of my (ENFJ) Front Seat activities:

- Take a walk in nature, being mindful while doing it
- Connect with a friend in person
- See clients
- Do good work
- Type someone
- Listen to fun, upbeat music
- Create something new
- Dance
- Get out of the house

Again, what are yours?

Ok, you get this? I sure hope so. This can (and will) seriously change your business when you can start identifying your Front Seat and your Back Seat. The goal is to spend at least 80% of your time in your business doing Front Seat activities and delegating almost, if not all, of your Drunk Uncle activities so you can avoid waking up the Baby in the Back Seat. As we continue to Section 3 (Mindset) and Section 4 (Taking Action), you will not be able to do them effectively if you are not in your Front Seat! In other words, if you are in your Back Seat, you will not be able to up-level your mindset and take effective action. So please, please, please find a way to start living your life from the Front Seat and stop doing things you suck at. Your business is on the line.

CHAPTER 13

Introverts: Your Car

I want there to be no confusion about how you need to be spending your time, where your best energy comes from, how ideal clients are going to be attracted to you, how you are going to make great money, and how you are going to kick ass in your business. I have outlined every car so you can clearly see your Front Seat awesomeness and your wonky Back Seat yuckiness.

ISTJ—The Duty Filler

Driver: Your Best Self

INTROVERTED SENSING IN THE INTERNAL WORLD/IN YOUR HEAD:

» You have an internal library of detailed personal knowledge, facts, feelings, sensations, and information gleaned from experiences.
» Your mind is like a vast internal storehouse of data, details, and impressions (internal file cabinet).
» You enjoy rituals and traditions like holidays and birthdays.
» You feel comfortable and happy with a day-to-day routine.
» You're big on details and data.

Drunk Uncle in the Back Seat
Things You Suck at and Should NOT Be Doing

FEELING:

» Dealing with other people's feelings.
» Having to explain/explore your values, beliefs and sense of self.
» Having to deal with or be sensitive to other people's emotions and inner sensations.
» Working in a capacity that requires you to be conciliatory or to create harmony with others.
» Doing work which requires you to work with deep internal feelings (yours or anyone else's).
» You need to have people in your life to help you see others' feelings since this is an area you are going to struggle with.

Copilot: Your Second-Best Self
(What the World Sees of You)

EXTROVERTED THINKING IN THE EXTERNAL WORLD:

» Order is important to you.
» You enjoy organizing both people and things to achieve a purpose.
» You use logic and reasoning with others.
» You direct action and make decisions.
» You are an impersonal decision maker.
» You collect information in an orderly way.
» You solve problems in a systematic manner.

Baby in the Back Seat
Highly Stressed from Doing Stuff You Suck At

EXTROVERTED INTUITION IN THE EXTERNAL WORLD YOU GET LOUD:

» You express your worries out loud.
» Every little thing becomes a huge deal.
» If you have a fight with your spouse, you think you are getting a divorce.
» You tell everyone what you imagine is going to happen next; the worse your expectation, the more you talk and the louder you get.

ISFJ—The Nurturer

Driver: Your Best Self

INTROVERTED SENSING IN THE INTERNAL WORLD/IN YOUR HEAD OR HEART:

- » You have an internal library of detailed personal knowledge, facts, feelings, sensations and information gleaned from experiences.
- » Your mind is like a vast internal storehouse of data, details and impressions (internal file cabinet).
- » You enjoy rituals and traditions like holidays and birthdays.
- » You feel comfortable and happy with a day-to-day routine.
- » You're big on details and data.

Drunk Uncle in the Back Seat: Things You Suck at and Should NOT Be Doing

THINKING:

- » Work that requires you to use strict logic and order.
- » Anything that doesn't recognize your intuitive wisdom.
- » Activities which require you to internally process and discriminate logic from illogic.
- » Work that requires you to seek clues and root causes, like a detective.
- » Having to solve other people's problems (often or repeatedly).
- » You need to have people in your life to help you see the logic in situations since this is an area you are going to struggle with.

Copilot: Your Second-Best Self
(What the World Sees of You)

EXTROVERTED FEELING IN THE EXTERNAL WORLD:

- » You reach out to attach and interact with other living things.
- » You nurture relationships and connections.
- » You validate and value others.
- » You're often found encouraging, coaching, educating, and motivating others.
- » You're good at protecting, helping, and caretaking.
- » You promote collaboration.
- » You seek harmony in interpersonal relationships.

Baby in the Back Seat:
Highly Stressed from Doing Things You Suck At

EXTROVERTED INTUITION IN THE EXTERNAL WORLD YOU GET LOUD:

- » You express your worries out loud.
- » Every little thing becomes a huge deal.
- » If you have a fight with your spouse, you think you are getting a divorce.
- » You tell everyone what you imagine is going to happen next; the worse your expectation, the more you talk and the louder you get.

INFJ—The Protector

Driver: Your Best Self

INTROVERTED INTUITION IN THE INTERNAL WORLD/IN YOUR HEART:

» You see patterns, relationships, symbols, meanings.
» You make magical connections to practical problems.
» You create a unique vision and arrive at unique insights about things or people.
» You can fill in the missing pieces of a life puzzle.
» You have complex visions or perspectives that you are unable to explain with clarity to others.
» You often ask yourself (and others) "What if…"
» You're always thinking about what's next or how you could be improving yourself or your situation.

Drunk Uncle in the Back Seat: Things You Suck at and Should NOT Be Doing

THINKING

» Work that requires you to use strict logic and order.
» Anything that doesn't recognize your intuitive wisdom.
» Activities which require you to internally process and discriminate logic from illogic.
» Work that requires you to seek clues and root causes, like a detective.
» Having to solve other people's problems (often or repeatedly).
» You need to have people in your life to help you see the logic in situations since this is an area you are going to struggle with.

Copilot: Your Second-Best Self
(What the World Sees of You)

EXTROVERTED FEELING IN THE EXTERNAL WORLD:

- » You reach out to attach and interact with other living things.
- » You nurture relationships and connections.
- » You validate and value others.
- » You're often found encouraging, coaching, educating, and motivating others.
- » You're good at protecting, helping, and caretaking.
- » You promote collaboration.
- » You seek harmony in interpersonal relationships.

Baby in the Back Seat:
Highly Stressed from Doing Things You Suck At

EXTROVERTED SENSING IN THE EXTERNAL WORLD:

- » You get loud and start bossing people around.
- » You start obsessing about details, facts.
- » You demand that people do things a very specific way.
- » You develop a "my way or the highway" mentality.
- » You might go into a list-making binge.
- » You want to talk about every detail of a conversation or the way a situation went (especially if it ended badly for you).
- » You may go on an eating, drinking, or exercise binge.

INTJ—The Scientist

Driver: Your Best Self

INTROVERTED INTUITION IN THE INTERNAL WORLD/IN YOUR HEAD:

» You see patterns, relationships, symbols, meanings.
» You make magical connections to practical problems.
» You create a unique vision and arrive at unique insights about things or people.
» You can fill in the missing pieces of a life puzzle
» You have complex visions or perspectives that you are unable to explain with clarity to others.
» You're always asking yourself (and others) "What if…"
» You always think about what's next or how you could be improving yourself or your situation.

Drunk Uncle in the Back Seat: Things You Suck at and Should NOT Be Doing

INTROVERTED FEELING IN THE INTERNAL WORLD/IN YOUR HEAD OR HEART:

» Dealing with other people's feelings.
» Having to explain/explore your values, beliefs and sense of self.
» Having to deal with or be sensitive to other people's emotions and inner sensations.
» Working in a capacity that requires you to be conciliatory or to create harmony with others.
» Doing work which requires you to work with deep internal feelings (yours or anyone else's).
» You need to have people in your life to help you see others' feelings since this is an area you are going to struggle with.

Copilot: Your Second-Best Self
(What the World Sees of You)

EXTROVERTED THINKING IN THE EXTERNAL WORLD:

- » Order is important to you.
- » Order the outside world.
- » You enjoy organizing both people and things to achieve a purpose.
- » You use logic and reasoning with others.
- » You direct action and make decisions.
- » You are an impersonal decision maker.
- » You collect information in an orderly way.
- » You solve problems in a systematic manner.

Baby in the Back Seat:
Highly Stressed from Doing Things You Suck At

EXTROVERTED SENSING IN THE EXTERNAL WORLD:

- » You get loud and start bossing people around.
- » You start obsessing about details, facts.
- » You demand that people do things a very specific way.
- » You develop a "my way or the highway" mentality.
- » You might go into a list-making binge.
- » You want to talk about every detail of a conversation or the way a situation went (especially if it ended badly for you).
- » You may go on an eating, drinking, or exercise binge.

ISTP—The Mechanic

Driver: Your Best Self

INTROVERTED THINKING IN THE INTERNAL WORLD/IN YOUR HEAD OR HEART:

» Logical order is what is most important to you.
» You will dismiss illogic; you will ignore the trivial.
» As you take in information, it is logically organized in your mind.
» You sort out and discriminate that which makes logical sense from that which does not.
» You are like a detective.
» You are a problem solver, seeking clues and root causes.

Drunk Uncle in the Back Seat: Things You Suck at and Should NOT Be Doing

INTROVERTED INTUITION IN THE INTERNAL WORLD/IN YOUR HEAD:

» Doing things which require you to see patterns, relationships, symbols, meanings.
» Trying to make magical connections to practical problems.
» When people expect you to just "understand" them when they don't make sense.
» Anything that requires you to fill in the missing pieces of a puzzle.
» Activities where you have to think or imagine "what's next".
» Activities which routinely ask you to imagine possibilities.
» You dislike all new-age, flakey, woo-woo stuff.
» You need to have people in your life to help you see possibilities and the big picture since this is an area you are going to struggle with.

Copilot: Your Second-Best Self
(What the World Sees of You)

EXTROVERTED SENSING IN THE EXTERNAL WORLD:

» You are good at seizing the moment and becoming immersed in the here and now.
» You pleasurably and spontaneously interact with people, things, and situations of interest.
» You are good at turning "work" into play.
» You enjoy learning by doing (touch it, taste it, hear it, smell it, see it).
» You enjoy new sensory experiences.
» You're big on details and data.
» You enjoy play.

Baby in the Back Seat:
Highly Stressed from Doing Things You Suck At

EXTROVERTED FEELING IN THE EXTERNAL WORLD:

» Your normal logical self goes away.
» You become intensely emotional.
» You may cry, scream, yell.
» Your outbursts may cause you to be "in people's faces"—this can scare them.

ISFP—The Artist

Driver: Your Best Self

INTROVERTED FEELING IN THE INTERNAL WORLD/IN YOUR HEAD OR HEART:

- You are incredibly sensitive.
- You are aware of and cherish your own values, beliefs, and sense of self.
- You are open to emotions and inner sensations.
- You are sensitive to others in an empathetic way.
- Authenticity is important to you.
- You seek harmony with others and harmony within.
- You have deep internal feelings.

Drunk Uncle in the Back Seat: Things You Suck at and Should NOT Be Doing

INTUITION:

- Doing things which require you to see patterns, relationships, symbols, meanings.
- Trying to make magical connections to practical problems.
- Expecting to just "understand" people when they don't make sense.
- Anything that requires you to fill in the missing pieces of a puzzle.
- Activities where you have to think or imagine "what's next".
- Activities which routinely ask you to imagine possibilities.
- You need to have people in your life to help you see possibilities and the big picture since this is an area you are going to struggle with.

Copilot: Your Second-Best Self
(What the World Sees of You)

EXTROVERTED SENSING IN THE EXTERNAL WORLD:

- » You are good at seizing the moment and becoming immersed in the here and now.
- » You pleasurably and spontaneously interact with people, things, and situations of interest.
- » You are good at turning "work" into play.
- » You enjoy learning by doing (touch it, taste it, hear it, smell it, see it).
- » You enjoy new sensory experiences.
- » You're big on details and data.
- » You enjoy play.

Baby in the Back Seat:
Highly Stressed from Doing Things You Suck At

EXTROVERTED THINKING IN THE EXTERNAL WORLD:

- » You shout and get in people's faces.
- » You become loud and bossy in the outside world.
- » You try to apply a systematic manner to solve problems.
- » You get out of your heart center and into your head.
- » You become cold and impersonal when dealing with people and making decisions.
- » Your friends will wonder if you got replaced by Spock.
- » You base everything on reason and logic.

INFP—The Idealist

Driver: Your Best Self

INTROVERTED FEELING IN THE INTERNAL WORLD/IN YOUR HEART:

» You are incredibly sensitive.
» You are aware of and cherish your own values, beliefs, and sense of self.
» You are open to emotions and inner sensations.
» You are sensitive to others in an empathetic way.
» Authenticity is important to you.
» You seek harmony with others and harmony within.
» You have deep internal feelings.

Drunk Uncle in the Back Seat: Things You Suck at and Should NOT Be Doing

SENSING

» Anything that requires you to be a virtual repository of data, details, and impressions.
» Having to remember people's birthdays, anniversaries, or other important milestones.
» Work that requires you to remember people and/or places and manage minute details and data on a regular basis.
» A job that is the same thing day in, day out since routine kills you.
» You need to have people in your life to help you see the facts and details since this is an area you are going to struggle with.

Copilot: Your Second-Best Self
(What the World Sees of You)

EXTROVERTED INTUITION IN THE EXTERNAL WORLD:

» You explore new ideas, people and possibilities.
» You are imaginative, inventive, and innovative.
» You see the big picture and future possibilities.
» You naturally energize people.
» You engage action towards a vision of what could be.
» You're always asking yourself "What if…"
» You are creative.
» You often think outside the box.
» 75% of people can't see what you see; you have a gift that others need.

Baby in the Back Seat:
Highly Stressed from Doing Things You Suck At

EXTROVERTED THINKING IN THE EXTERNAL WORLD:

» You shout and get in people's faces.
» You become loud and bossy in the outside world.
» You try to apply a systematic manner to solve problems.
» You get out of your heart center and into your head.
» You become cold and impersonal when dealing with people and making decisions.
» Your friends will wonder if you got replaced by Spock.
» You base everything on reason and logic.

INTP—The Thinker

Driver: Your Best Self

INTROVERTED THINKING IN THE INTERNAL WORLD/IN YOUR HEAD OR HEART:

» Logical order is what is most important to you.
» You will dismiss illogic; you will ignore the trivial.
» As you take in information, it is logically organized in your mind.
» You sort out and discriminate that which makes logical sense from that which does not.
» You are like a detective.
» You are a problem-solver, seeking clues and root causes.

Drunk Uncle in the Back Seat: Things You Suck at and Should NOT Be Doing

SENSING

» Anything that requires you to be a virtual repository of data, details, and impressions.
» Having to remember people's birthdays, anniversaries, or other important milestones.
» Work that requires you to remember people and/or places with minute details and data on a regular basis.
» A job that is the same thing day in, day out, since routine kills you.
» You need to have people in your life to help you see the facts and details since this is an area you are going to struggle with.

Copilot: Your Second-Best Self
(What the World Sees of You)

EXTROVERTED INTUITION IN THE EXTERNAL WORLD:

- » You explore new ideas, new people, and possibilities.
- » You are imaginative, inventive, and innovative.
- » You see the big picture and future possibilities.
- » You naturally energize people.
- » You engage action towards a vision of what could be.
- » You're always asking yourself "What if…"
- » You are creative.
- » You often think outside the box.
- » 75% of people can't see what you see; you have a gift that others need.

Baby in the Back Seat:
Highly Stressed from Doing Things You Suck At

EXTROVERTED FEELING IN THE EXTERNAL WORLD:

- » Your normal logical self goes away.
- » You become overly emotional, perhaps even hysterical.
- » You may cry, scream, yell.
- » You become confrontational and "in their face" when people upset you.

Extroverts: Your car

*You can tell when people are truly happy.
Their energy is genuine.*

—ALEX ELLE

Driver
is an Extrovert. You give your best self to the world.

Copilot
is an Introvert.

Drunk Uncle in the back seat
Don't do extroverted or introverted stuff you suck at.

Baby in the backseat
is Introverted.

ESTP—The Doer

Driver: Your Best Self
(What the World Sees of You)

EXTROVERTED SENSING IN THE EXTERNAL WORLD:

» You seize the moment and become immersed in the here and now.
» You pleasurably and spontaneously interact with people, things, and situations of interest.
» You're good at turning "work" into play.
» You enjoy learning by doing (touch it, taste it, hear it, smell it, see it).
» You enjoy sensory experiences.
» Details and data are the way that you take in information and process it.
» You are playful.

Drunk Uncle in the Back Seat:
Things You Suck at and Should NOT Be Doing

FEELING

» Forcing yourself to reach out to attach and interact with other living things.
» Trying to nurture relationships, make connections, or promote collaboration.
» Being involved in activities which require you to validate and value others.
» Activities where you must encourage, coach, educate, or motivate.
» Things that require you to act in a protecting, helping, and caretaking capacity.
» Being in situations that require you to seek harmony in interpersonal relationships.
» You need to have people in your life to help you see others' feelings since this is an area you are going to struggle with.

Copilot: Your Second-Best Self

INTROVERTED THINKING IN THE INTERNAL WORLD/IN YOUR HEAD:

- » Logical order rules all.
- » Illogic is dismissed as trivial.
- » Information is taken in and logically organized in your mind.
- » You sort out and discriminate that which makes logical sense from that which does not.
- » You are like a detective.
- » You are a problem-solver, seeking clues and root causes.

Baby in the Back Seat: Highly Stressed from Doing Things You Suck At

INTROVERTED INTUITION IN THE INTERNAL WORLD YOU GET QUIET:

- » You hide in your home, away from friends and family.
- » You isolate yourself.
- » Internally you worry.
- » Every little thing becomes a huge deal.
- » If you have a fight with your spouse, you think you are getting a divorce.
- » You start imagining every possible bad thing that can happen to you or your situation.

ESFP—The Performer

Driver: Your Best Self
(What the World Sees of You)

EXTROVERTED SENSING IN THE EXTERNAL WORLD:

» You are good at seizing the moment and becoming immersed in the here and now.
» You pleasurably and spontaneously interact with people, things, and situations of interest.
» You're good at turning "work" into play.
» You enjoy learning by doing (touch it, taste it, hear it, smell it, see it).
» You enjoy sensory experiences.
» Details and data are your foundation for your experience and knowledge.
» You are playful.

Drunk Uncle in the Back Seat:
Things You Suck at and Should NOT Be Doing

FEELING IN THE

» Things that require you to use logic and reasoning with others.
» Activities that require you to organize people and things to achieve a purpose.
» Projects where you must make impersonal decisions, take direct action, and be impersonal.
» Things where you must collect information in an orderly way or solve problems in a systematic manner.
» You need to have people in your life to help you see logic and reasoning since this is an area you are going to struggle with.

Copilot: Your Second-Best Self

INTROVERTED FEELING IN THE INTERNAL WORLD/IN YOUR HEAD OR HEART:

- » You are very sensitive.
- » You're aware of and cherish your own values, beliefs, and sense of self.
- » You are open to emotions and inner sensations.
- » You are sensitive to others in an empathetic way.
- » Authenticity is important to you.
- » You seek harmony with others and harmony within.
- » You have and experience deep internal feelings.

Baby in the Back Seat: Highly Stressed from Doing Things You Suck At

INTROVERTED INTUITION IN THE INTERNAL WORLD YOU GET QUIET:

- » You retreat from the world.
- » You go inward.
- » You internalize your worry.
- » Every little thing becomes a huge deal.
- » If you have a fight with your spouse, you think you are getting a divorce.
- » You imagine every possible bad thing that could happen to you or a situation.

ENFP—The Inspirer

Driver: Your Best Self
(What the World Sees of You)

EXTROVERTED INTUITION IN THE EXTERNAL WORLD:

» You explore new ideas, new people and possibilities.
» You are imaginative, inventive, and innovative.
» You naturally energize people.
» You engage action towards a vision of what could be.
» You see future possibilities and the big picture.
» You're a what-if'er.
» You're creative and think outside the box.
» 75% of people can't see what you see; you have a gift that others need.

Drunk Uncle in the Back Seat:
Things You Suck at and Should NOT Be Doing

THINKING:

» Things that require you to use logic and reasoning with others.
» Activities that require you to organize people and things to achieve a purpose.
» Projects where you must make impersonal decisions, direct action, and be impersonal.
» Things where you must collect information in an orderly way or solve problems in a systematic manner.
» You need to have people in your life to help you see logic and reasoning since this is an area you are going to struggle with.

Copilot: Your Second-Best Self

INTROVERTED FEELING IN THE INTERNAL WORLD/IN YOUR HEART:

- You are very sensitive.
- You are aware of and cherish your own values, beliefs, and sense of self.
- You are open to emotions and inner sensations.
- You are sensitive to others in an empathetic way.
- Authenticity is important to you.
- You seek harmony with others and harmony within.
- You have deep internal feelings.

Baby in the Back Seat: Highly Stressed from Doing Things You Suck At

INTROVERTED SENSING IN THE INTERNAL WORLD/IN YOUR HEAD OR HEART:

- You retreat into your own personal world.
- You internally obsess about details, facts.
- You might go over every detail of a conversation or the way a situation went in your head.
- Your head feels wonky, and you feel horrible.
- You go on a list-making binge.
- You might go on a food, drink, or exercise binge.

ENTP—The Visionary

Driver: Your Best Self
(What the World Sees of You)

EXTROVERTED INTUITION IN THE EXTERNAL WORLD:

- » You explore new ideas, people, and possibilities.
- » You are imaginative, inventive, and innovative.
- » You naturally energize people.
- » You engage action towards a vision of what could be.
- » You see future possibilities and the big picture.
- » You're a what-if'er.
- » You're creative and think outside the box.
- » 75% of people can't see what you see; you have a gift that others need.

Drunk Uncle in the Back Seat:
Things You Suck at and Should NOT Be Doing

FEELING:

- » Forcing yourself to reach out to attach and interact with other living things.
- » Trying to nurture relationships, make connections, or promote collaboration.
- » Activities which require you to validate and value others.
- » Activities where you must encourage, coach, educate, or motivate.
- » Things that require you to act in a protecting, helping, and caretaking capacity.
- » Be in situations that require you to seek harmony in interpersonal relationships.
- » You need to have people in your life to help you see others' feelings since this is an area you are going to struggle with.

Copilot: Your Second-Best Self

INTROVERTED THINKING IN THE INTERNAL WORLD/IN YOUR HEAD OR HEART:

- » In your life, logic and order rule.
- » You dismiss anything illogical as being trivial.
- » You take in information and logically organize it in your mind.
- » You sort out and discriminate that which makes logical sense from that which does not.
- » You are like a detective.
- » You problem-solve, seeking clues and root causes.

Baby in the Back Seat: Highly Stressed from Doing Things You Suck At

INTROVERTED SENSING IN THE INTERNAL WORLD/IN YOUR HEAD OR HEART:

- » You retreat into your personal world.
- » You internally obsess about details, facts.
- » You might go on a list-making binge.
- » You go over every detail of a conversation or the way a situation went in your head.
- » You exude horrible, wonky, quiet, in your head energy that people do not like.
- » You may overeat, overdrink or overexercise.

ESTJ—The Guardian

Driver: Your Best Self
(What the World Sees of You)

EXTROVERTED THINKING IN THE EXTERNAL WORLD:

» You are happy when everything is in order.
» You organize both people and things to achieve a purpose.
» You use logic and reasoning with others.
» You direct action and make impersonal decisions.
» You collect information in an orderly way.
» You solve problems in a systematic manner.

Drunk Uncle in the Back Seat:
Things You Suck at and Should NOT Be Doing

INTUITION:

» Forcing yourself to explore new ideas, people, and possibilities.
» Forcing yourself to be more imaginative, inventive, and innovative.
» Trying to see the big picture.
» Trying to energize people.
» Seeing what possibilities may exist in the future.
» Playing "what if" games with Intuitive Types.
» Trying to think outside the box.
» You need to have people in your life to help you see possibilities and alternatives since this is an area you are going to struggle with.

Copilot: Your Second-Best Self

INTROVERTED SENSING IN THE INTERNAL WORLD/IN YOUR HEAD OR HEART:

» You have an internal library of detailed personal knowledge, facts, feelings, sensations, and information gleaned from experiences.
» You have an internal storehouse of data and details (internal file cabinet).
» You enjoy rituals and traditions like holidays and birthdays.
» Day-to-day routine makes you happy.
» You're a stickler for details and data.

Baby in the Back Seat: Highly Stressed from Doing Things You Suck At

INTROVERTED FEELING IN THE INTERNAL WORLD/IN YOUR HEAD OR HEART:

» You retreat from the world.
» You may not want to get out of bed.
» You feel overwhelmed by your emotions.
» You feel deeply hurt.
» Your emotionally distraught and withdrawn behavior worries people in your life.

ESFJ—The Caregiver

Driver: Your Best Self
(What the World Sees of You)

EXTROVERTED FEELING IN THE EXTERNAL WORLD:

» You reach out to attach and interact with other living things.
» You nurture relationships and connections.
» You validate and value others.
» You encourage, coach, educate, and motivate.
» You protect, help, and take care of people and things.
» You're all about collaboration.
» You seek harmony in interpersonal relationships.

Drunk Uncle in the Back Seat:
Things You Suck at and Should NOT Be Doing

INTUITION:

» Forcing yourself to explore new ideas, people, and possibilities.
» Forcing yourself to be more imaginative, inventive, and innovative.
» Trying to see the big picture.
» Trying to energize people.
» Seeing what possibilities may exist in the future.
» Playing "what if" games with Intuitive Types.
» Trying to think outside the box.
» You need to have people in your life to help you see possibilities and alternatives since this is an area you are going to struggle with.

Copilot: Your Second-Best Self

INTROVERTED SENSING IN THE INTERNAL WORLD/IN YOUR HEART:

» You have an internal library of detailed personal knowledge, facts, feelings, sensations, and information gleaned from experiences.
» You have a vast internal storehouse of data, details, and impressions (internal file cabinet).
» You enjoy rituals and traditions like holidays and birthdays.
» You thrive in a day-to-day routine.
» You're a stickler for details and data.

Baby in the Back Seat: Highly Stressed from Doing Things You Suck At

INTROVERTED THINKING IN THE INTERNAL WORLD/IN YOUR HEAD OR HEART:

» You hide from the world.
» You might obsessively go over details, facts, and data in your head.
» You abandon your normal Extroverted Feeling self and retreat into your thoughts.
» You may not want to leave the house or be around people.
» You internally process logic and data over and over.
» You feel icky and gross, as if you have lost your mojo.
» You repel people by being in your head and not your heart.

ENFJ—The Giver

Driver: Your Best Self
(What the World Sees of You)

EXTROVERTED FEELING IN THE EXTERNAL WORLD:

» You reach out to attach and interact with other living things.
» You nurture relationships and connections.
» You validate and value others.
» You encourage, coach, educate, and motivate.
» You protect, help, and take care of others.
» You promote collaboration.
» You seek harmony in interpersonal relationships.

Drunk Uncle in the Back Seat:
Things You Suck at and Should NOT Be Doing

SENSING

» Trying to live in the moment and immersing yourself in the here and now.
» Trying to interact spontaneously with people, things and situations of interest.
» Trying to turn work into play.
» Managing details and data.
» Trying to learn by doing (touch it, taste it, hear it, smell it, see it).
» Having only sensory experiences.
» You need to have people in your life to help you see facts, data, and details since this is an area you are going to struggle with.

Copilot: Your Second-Best Self

INTROVERTED INTUITION IN THE INTERNAL WORLD/IN YOUR HEAD OR HEART:

- » You see patterns, relationships, symbols, meanings.
- » You make magical connections to practical problems.
- » You create a unique vision and arrive at unique insights about things or people.
- » You can fill in the missing pieces of a life puzzle.
- » You have complex visions or perspectives that you are unable to explain with clarity to others.
- » You're always thinking "what if".
- » You always think about what's next or how you could be improving yourself or your situation.

Baby in the Back Seat: Highly Stressed from Doing Things You Suck At

INTROVERTED THINKING IN THE INTERNAL WORLD/IN YOUR HEAD:

- » You hide from the world.
- » You obsessively go over details, facts, and data in your head.
- » You abandon your normal Extroverted Feeling self and retreat into your own world in your head.
- » You may not want to leave the house.
- » You don't want to be around people.
- » You process logic data over and over again in your head.
- » You have horrible energy, and it seems as if you have lost your mojo.
- » You repel people by being in your head and not your heart.

ENTJ—The Executive

Driver: Your Best Self
(What the World Sees of You)

EXTROVERTED THINKING IN THE EXTERNAL WORLD:

» Your focus is order.
» You organize both people and things to achieve a purpose.
» You use logic and reasoning with others.
» You are all about direct action.
» You are an impersonal decision maker.
» You call plays and make decisions.
» You collect information in an orderly way.
» You solve problems in a systematic manner.

Drunk Uncle in the Back Seat:
Things You Suck at and Should NOT Be Doing

SENSING

» Trying to live in the moment and immersing yourself in the here and now.
» Trying to interact spontaneously with people, things and situations of interest.
» Trying to turn work into play.
» Managing details and data.
» Trying to learn by doing (touch it, taste it, hear it, smell it, see it).
» Having only sensory experiences.
» You need to have people in your life to help you see facts, data and details since this is an area you are going to struggle with.

Copilot: Your Second-Best Self

INTROVERTED INTUITION IN THE INTERNAL WORLD/IN YOUR HEAD OR HEART:

» You see patterns, relationships, symbols, meanings.
» You make magical connections to practical problems.
» You create a unique vision, and arrive at unique insights about things or people.
» You can fill in the missing pieces of a life puzzle.
» You have complex visions or perspectives that you are unable to explain with clarity to others.
» You're a what-if'er.
» You're always thinking about what's next or how you could be improving yourself or your situation.

Baby in the Back Seat: Highly Stressed from Doing Things You Suck At

INTROVERTED FEELING IN THE INTERNAL WORLD/IN YOUR HEART:

» You withdraw from the world.
» You may not want to get out of bed.
» You have deep, hurt feelings.
» You feel overwhelmed by emotions.
» When you behave so emotionally, withdrawn and distraught, it worries the people in your life.

Summary of Front Seat Activities

To achieve true greatness in your business, you must spend at least 80% of your time in your Front Seat as the Driver and Copilot. Your best energy and your best self show up when you're in the Front Seat. *Here's a review of Front Seat experiences:*

Intuitives (N)

Extroverted Intuition

IN THE EXTERNAL WORLD:

- You explore new ideas, people and possibilities.
- You are imaginative, inventive, and innovative.
- You think and see the big picture.
- You naturally energize people.
- You engage in action towards a vision of what could be.
- You entertain future possibilities.
- You're a "what-if'er."
- You are creative.
- You think outside the box.

Remember that 75% of people can't see what you see; you have a gift that others need!

Introverted Intuition

IN THE INTERNAL WORLD/IN YOUR HEAD OR HEART:

- You see patterns, relationships, symbols, meanings.
- You make magical connections to practical problems.
- You create a unique vision and arrive at unique insights about things or people.
- You can fill in the missing pieces of a life puzzle.
- You have complex visions or perspectives that you are unable to explain with clarity to others.
- You like to ask, "What if?"
- You always think about what's next or how you could be improving yourself or your situation.

Sensors (S)

Extroverted Sensing

IN THE EXTERNAL WORLD:

- You seize the moment and become immersed in the here and now.
- You pleasurably and spontaneously interact with people, things, and situations of interest.
- You're good at turning work into play.
- You learn by doing (touch it, taste it, hear it, smell it, see it).
- You enjoy sensory experiences.
- You easily manipulate and process details and data.
- You like doing things with your hands.
- You are playful.

Introverted Sensing

IN THE INTERNAL WORLD/IN YOUR HEAD OR HEART:

- You have an internal library of detailed personal knowledge, facts, feelings, sensations, and information gleaned from experiences.
- You have a vast internal storehouse of data, details, and impressions (internal file cabinet).
- You enjoy rituals and traditions like holidays and birthdays.
- You're good at day-to-day routine.
- You manage details and data well.

Feelers (F)

Extroverted Feeling

IN THE EXTERNAL WORLD:

- You reach out to attach and interact with other living things.
- You nurture relationships; you validate and value others.
- You value connections.
- You encourage, coach, educate, and motivate.
- You protect, help, and take care of others.
- You promote collaboration.
- You seek harmony in interpersonal relationships.

Introverted Feeling

IN THE INTERNAL WORLD/IN YOUR HEAD OR HEART:

- You are the most sensitive of all the Types.
- You are aware of and cherish your own values, beliefs, and sense of self.
- You are open to emotions and inner sensations.
- You are sensitive to others in an empathetic way.
- Being authentic is important to you.
- You seek harmony with others and harmony within.
- You have deep internal feelings.

Thinkers (T)

Extroverted Thinking

IN THE EXTERNAL WORLD:

- Your focus is order.
- You organize both people and things to achieve a purpose.
- You use logic and reasoning with others.
- You're the "director" in life.
- You're an impersonal decision maker.
- You call plays and make decisions.
- You collect information in an orderly way.
- You solve problems in a systematic manner.

Introverted Thinking

IN THE INTERNAL WORLD/IN YOUR HEAD OR HEART:

- Logical order rules all.
- You dismiss illogic as trivial.
- Information is taken in and logically organized in your mind.
- You sort out and discriminate that which makes logical sense from that which does not.
- You are like a detective.
- You are a problem-solver, seeking clues and root causes.

Summary of Drunk Uncle in the Back Seat

As I hope I have made clear, to have a truly successful business you love and make a great living at, it is critical that you stop doing the things you suck at—spending less than 20% of your time in the Back Seat. Based on your type, when you do these things, it is like a drunk person doing them. Whether your energy is introverted or extroverted with all other passengers of the car, when it comes to the Drunk Uncle, it doesn't matter; I want you to stop doing these behaviors altogether!

If your Drunk Uncle is an Intuitive, here is a list of the things you suck at:

Intuitives (N)
Extroverted or Introverted Intuition

You suck at:

- Exploring new ideas, new people and possibilities.
- Being imaginative, inventive, and innovative.
- Seeing the big picture.
- Playing with future possibilities.
- Thinking outside the box; you would rather do it the way it has already been done before.
- Hearing "woo-woo" talk.
- Seeing patterns, relationships, symbols, meanings.
- Filling in the missing pieces of a life puzzle.

If your Drunk Uncle is a Sensor, here is a list of the things you suck at:

Sensors (S)
Extroverted or Introverted Sensing

You suck at:

- Details, data, facts.
- Seizing the moment and becoming immersed in the here and now.
- Turning work into play.

- Living in the moment.
- Day-to-day routine.
- Giving necessary data to people in your life who need it.
- Remembering important dates like holidays and birthdays.

If your Drunk Uncle is a Feeler, here is a list of the things you suck at:

Feelers (F)
Extroverted or Introverted Feeling

You suck at:

- Reaching out to attach and interact with other living things.
- Nurturing relationships.
- Validating others' feelings.
- Promoting collaboration.
- Seeking harmony in interpersonal relationships.
- Being sensitive to others and your own feelings.
- Empathy in work situations or when making decisions.
- Accessing deep internal feelings.

If your Drunk Uncle is an Thinker, here is a list of the things you suck at:

Thinkers (T)
Extroverted or Introverted Thinking

You suck at:

- Impersonal logic or reasoning.
- Organizing both people and things to achieve a purpose.
- Making impersonal decisions.
- Solving problems in a systematic manner.
- Logically organizing information in your mind.
- Sorting out and discriminating that which makes logical sense from that which does not.
- Problem-solving, seeking clues and seeing root causes.

Summary of Baby in the Back Seat

Inevitably, when we are running our own businesses and all that comes along with being an entrepreneur, your Baby in the Back Seat is going to show up. You just have to be aware of when the little one is present. Sometimes, you should even allow your Baby to stick around for a while, but only a short while so you can get back to doing your authentic work in your business and with your clients. But when the tantrum is over, get back in your Front Seat by doing the activities that will put you there.

Introverted Baby in the Back Seat

Remember, Introvert Drivers are normally rather quiet, somewhat reserved, docile, and even-tempered. But when their Babies wake up, they get loud, in your face, and act out in the ways described below.

Extroverted Intuition

IN THE EXTERNAL WORLD, YOU GET LOUD:

- Externally, you worry.
- Every little thing becomes a huge deal.
- If you have a fight with your spouse, you think you are getting a divorce.
- You imagine every little thing that could go wrong.
- Everything is a catastrophe.

Extroverted Sensing

IN THE EXTERNAL WORLD:

- You get loud and start bossing people around.
- You obsess about details, facts.
- You demand that people do things a very specific way.
- Your way or the highway thinking and way of dealing with people.
- You go into obsessive list-making mode.
- You will want to talk about every detail of a conversation or the way a situation went.
- You might overeat, overdrink or overexercise.

Extroverted Feeling

IN THE EXTERNAL WORLD, YOU GET LOUD:

- Your normal logical self goes away.
- You become overly emotional.
- You may cry, scream, yell.
- Logic goes away and is replaced with uncontrolled emotion, hysterics.
- You get in people's faces and it can scare them.

Extroverted Thinking

IN THE EXTERNAL WORLD, YOU GET LOUD:

- You get loud and in people's faces.
- You begin bossing people and things around in the outside world.
- You become impersonal when dealing with people and making decisions.
- You try to solve problems in a systematic manner.
- You get out of your heart (your happy place) and into your head.
- Your normally loving, caring personality becomes cold and logical.

Extroverted Baby in the Back Seat

Remember, Extroverts are normally out in the world connecting, being social, and sharing themselves. However, when their Babies wake up, they hide from the world and may have the thoughts or behaviors listed below.

Introverted Intuition

IN THE INTERNAL WORLD, YOU GET QUIET:

- You retreat from the world.
- You internalize your worry.
- You imagine every possible thing that could go wrong.
- Every little thing becomes a huge deal.
- If you have a fight with your spouse, you think you are getting a divorce.

Introverted Sensing

IN THE INTERNAL WORLD, YOU GET QUIET:

- You hide from the world and retreat into your own personal world.
- You internally obsess about details, facts.
- You go over every detail of a conversation or the way a situation went in your head.
- You obsessively go into list-making mode.
- You give off horrible, wonky, quiet, in your head energy that people do not like.
- You may overeat, overdrink, or overexercise.

Introverted Feeling

IN THE INTERNAL WORLD, YOU GET QUIET AND IN YOUR HEART:

- You hide, retreat from the world.
- You may not want to get out of bed.
- You feel very emotional and experience deep, hurt feelings.
- You feel overwhelmed by emotions.
- People worry to see you so emotional, distraught, and withdrawn.

Introverted Thinking

IN THE INTERNAL WORLD, YOU GET QUIET AND IN YOUR HEAD:

- You hide from the world.
- You obsessively go over details, facts, and data in your head.
- You abandon your normal Extroverted Feeling self and retreat into your own world in your head.
- You may not want to leave the house.
- You don't want to be around people.
- You process logic data over and over in your head.
- You feel like you've lost your mojo, energy, and zip for life.
- You repel people by being in your head and not your heart.

CHAPTER 14

The Trunk of Our Cars

"People with a high level of personal mastery are acutely aware of their ignorance, their incompetence, and their growth areas. And they are deeply self-confident."

—PETER SENGE, *THE FIFTH DISCIPLINE*

We are coming to the close of the second section, and I want you to check in with yourself. How are you feeling? Validated? Excited? Amazed? I know I experienced all of those emotions when I learned about personality Type. I was fresh out of college, in my first corporate job, when I discovered this life-changing information.

Over the last 25 years I have used my experience with Type, my skills and education as a therapist, and my own failed marriage to build a business from nothing to a thriving organization, which includes a successful coaching, speaking, and training business on Front Seat Life, Front Seat Life Business and soon to come, Front Seat Life Relationships. I hope you can take this and use it in your life every single day. I also want you to use this in your business every single day as it is what has propelled me and my amazing clients to success and happiness. Living a life of authenticity makes all that possible. I want you to use the language provided by Myers-Briggs and me (Driver, Copilot, Drunk Uncle in the Back Seat, and Baby in the Back Seat) to transform your life, your business, and your relationships.

Before I close the *Who Are You?* section, I have to talk briefly about that junk in our Back Seats that has nothing to do with our innate selves, but is garbage we have picked up along the way. It is going to be a bit of an abrupt change, but absolutely necessary if you are truly going to excel in your business.

Your Type and your innateness cannot and should not change. However, your nurtured self is an accumulation of all the things that have happened *to* you over time and make up a huge part of who you are.

There are influences that take each one of us away from being our innate selves—the people we were born into this world to be. We must stop fighting against this! I promise that this alone—ending the fight—will change your life. During my years as a therapist, I saw the effects of these nurtured issues every day in everyone, including business owners. We are our businesses and therefore if our lives are a mess, we can't give our best selves to our work either. I am going to put my therapist hat on for a minute. I would like you to think about Maslow's Hierarchy of Needs. At the bottom of the pyramid are basic survival skills. We need to have these things in order before we can move up the pyramid to self-actualization, which is where all the good, juicy, creative, amazing things happen. As much as we don't want to address certain issues in our lives, as business owners we must do so if we want to grow and evolve into authentic people that our clients can gravitate towards. In my work with clients, I combine two elements—counseling and coaching—to truly help them live more fulfilling lives as they learn to know themselves, identify their past patterns and ways of being and thinking, change the beliefs that no longer served them, and take action. I want the same for you.

As I mentioned at the beginning of this section, our nurtured self is the person who has developed in response to the environment in which they lived. This version of ourselves is a result of many factors, including family of origin (FOO), culture of origin (COO), traumas, birth order, and even unspoken roles and rules within the family. I call this big package of stuff "the trunks of our cars." Sometimes we never open the trunk of the car and examine how this stuff affects us, which keeps us stuck and not moving forward.

There is a huge myth out there—that if we don't talk about our stuff, it will go away. And while it may be true that our mess is our message, if we are constantly trying to hide our mess or run from it, we can't show up and be fully and authentically ourselves.

I am here to tell you the exact opposite is true. We must talk about the stuff in our trunks that happened to us throughout our lives because whether we like it or not, it affects who we are and how we show up in this world. There is a saying in Alcoholics Anonymous: secrets keep you sick. I have found that to be 100% true. The less we talk about something, the more it binds us, keeps us down, and keeps us sick.

There is another saying: "The truth will set you free." I have also found that to be true. We must accept what has happened to us in our lives and open up our trunk every once in a while to acknowledge that stuff is in there. Each time we open it up and talk about it, it loses its control over us. It is a powerful and true phenomenon.

We so often go through life with these burdens and wonder why on earth we're feeling overwhelmed and heavy. We forget to open the trunk, see what's inside, and ditch the junk that's been cluttering our lives and holding us back—or at least to come to terms with what's there. This stuff can also put us in our Back Seats, specifically as the Baby in the Back Seat, and it is time to start living our lives from the Front Seat. Therefore, we have to deal with some of this crap.

In this next part, we're going to explore all the different compartments in your trunk. Hopefully, this will help you feel like the trunk isn't so full or unwieldy anymore, because you are meant to be living your life from your Front Seat—not how someone else told you how to live your life.

What's in the Trunk of Your Car?

You may have seen that car driving down the street that clearly has so much stuff in the trunk it can't get up to speed. The crap in the trunk is bogging it down. Sometimes the trunk is so full and heavy that the car is no longer able to move. We are just like that! We have so much holding us down that we have a hard time moving forward in our lives. Codependency is one of the issues that shows up because of the crap in the trunk of our cars.

While where we come from doesn't define us, it does make up a huge part of who we are, whether we like it or not. As you work through this, you will start to see patterns in your life and in your relationships.

Who We're "Supposed" to Be

Within families, we are often forced to be someone we're not. Parents don't usually do this on purpose; they just don't know who they are, so they don't know how to allow you to be you either. We are often not allowed to be who we are, if that is different than our family, because it makes them uncomfortable.

There are many Intuitive Types out there who grew up feeling weird and misunderstood, or suppressing these creative urges because their parents didn't know what to do with them. Society tells girls they are supposed to be sweet and sensitive, but what if you are a Thinking woman and that just never felt like you? In your business, are you showing up inauthentically because you are a Thinking woman trying to fit into the world of Feeling women or can you just be unapologetically who you are and allow the right clients to find you?

Or you are a Feeling man who grew up with a Thinking mother, and you two just never quite connected and so you felt strange and different? Your family's Type can affect how you felt growing up. If you are one of the marginalized Types, it could have left you feeling like there was something wrong with you or like you needed to change to fit in. I believe what makes you weird is actually your greatest asset! I also believe that your mess is your message. But instead trying to be "normal," why not be your weird awesome self and attract the clients that actually like that? I promise you they are out there and they cannot find you if you are trying to be normal and just like everyone else. Bah, how boring.

This happened to me many times throughout my entire life, up until the past couple of years. I always wondered what was wrong with me until I finally realized that I grew up in a strong family of Sensors, then married a Sensor. I felt different because I *was* different from everyone I had spent most of my life with. When I started meeting other Intuitive Types through networking with entrepreneurial women, I realized these women were like me! I started to embrace my Intuitiveness and really started to grow. My weirdness became my greatest asset in my business! In fact, I created my entire business around the pain of growing up an Intuitive in a Sensing world. Since 97% of my clients are Intuitives, they wouldn't know how to find me if I hadn't decided to just be me and screw what everyone else thought. You ready to do the same with me?

However small, these traumas become the stuff we carry around in the trunks of our cars. They are the part of our childhood when we weren't allowed to be who we are. Sometimes these children aren't being allowed to be who they are because certain personality Types dominate the household or because of their religious background. No matter the reason why this occurs, these are considered traumas in the psyche and affect how we interact with others.

Most of my clients have experienced this type of personal suppression in their families, but one client in particular comes to mind; we will call her Connie. Connie grew up in a great household—loving parents, one sister, educated, middle class, what most everyone would wish for in a family of origin. Both her parents and sister were strong Extroverts, and Connie, as an Introvert, always felt like she wasn't able to keep up with the energy of her outgoing, domineering family. All three were also strong Sensing Types and expected Connie to get the grades her sister did, although because Connie is extremely smart as a strong Intuitive Type, she didn't do well in traditional schooling with standardized tests, so she always felt less-than and ended up not going to college because she believed she couldn't keep up. Connie is also the only Feeler in her family of Thinkers, which made her feel overly emotional and flakey compared to her logical family. And lastly, Connie is a strong P, a dreamer, a gypsy, and her entire family, until today, made her feel like a loser and a flake for choosing her own unique life path. She spent 30+ years living a life for them until she finally realized how miserable she was, and since then has decided to change her life to live it for her INFP Type. She now lives with a man who accepts her and is a successful author, truly living as an INFP and she couldn't be happier (even though her family still doesn't agree with her life). I tell you Connie's story so you can see that trauma doesn't have to be something like abuse in order for it to affect our entire lives. Our family of origin is often the first source of trauma in our life. It is important to acknowledge it, to know where that limiting belief comes from, thank it, and then go out and kick ass. It has kept you down long enough. No more.

Codependency

Many of you are likely in some form of a codependent relationship, and it is critically important to learn how you are playing this game with people in your life so you can stop that unhealthy behavior. I want to show you what codependency looks like so you can start to "stay on your side of the net." As you start to live your authentic life and Live Your Life from the Front Seat, you may experience some pushback from people in your life. As we grow our businesses, staying on our side of the net is critical for growing a successful team so we can show up authentically and unapologetically who we are as we work with clients.

I hope you are seeing yourself in a whole new way and are excited to start Living Your Life from the Front Seat so that you can once and for all stop doing stuff you suck at now that you know how serious it can be if you don't. You now know something new, different, and powerful about yourself that you cannot un-know. So the only thing to do now is live your life accordingly. Sometimes changes need to happen in our relationships in order to make that shift.

It's likely that this is going to challenge you, your relationships, and your belief system, but it can also set you free and make you much, much happier!

I want you to imagine a tennis court. There are two people on the tennis court, playing a game together. Each side of the net is each person's own territory, or their side of the net. They are responsible for it—to take care of it, make sure it is healthy, happy, and secure. It is where you are allowed to have your own opinions, beliefs, and personality type. We all need to manage our own side of the net in order to be in healthy relationships.

But what happens in almost all unhealthy or codependent relationships is you'll do one of two things:

1) You jump on the other side of the net to manage and control people or things.
2) Alternately, you allow other people to come into your court, on your side of the net to manage and control you. You lose your voice.

In my experience, Feeling (F) and Perceiving (P) Types have a tendency to be more of the codependent type that allows others to jump on your side of the net and manage and control you.

Thinking (T) and Judging (J) Types have more of a tendency to be the codependent type to jump on the other side of the net and manage and control other people.

Both of those situations are codependent behavior, and it is not healthy for you or your business. This shows that you are not comfortable knowing who you are, standing up for yourself, having a voice, and managing your own side of the net. If you want to run a truly successful business, you have to learn that not everyone is like you; they have their own talents and abilities. Let them be if they are doing good work, even if it may not be your way. Or you may need to grow a pair, start standing up for yourself, and don't be walked on.

When we are not comfortable with ourselves or don't know who we are, we are more likely to try to manage or control others or allow others to control us. Now that you know your type and are hopefully starting to Live Your Life from the Front Seat™, you can start the process of becoming healthily detached and not codependent. You can start to design your own side of the net, find your voice, know what you are great at, become comfortable with who you are, and run a business that makes you happy and proud. You will have no need to control others or be controlled when you can do that.

Healthy detachment looks like two people in any relationship having their own feelings, opinions, ideas, and lives while trusting the other person to do the same. There is no need to manage or control the other person because your own life is under control and you trust the other person to have control over their own. You must learn to hire people like that into your team. Even if you can't trust the other person to do so, you must learn how to get back on your side of the net and only manage and control yourself! You cannot control another person; you can only control yourself.

Viktor Frankl talks about this in his epic book, *Man's Search for Meaning*. There is a space for personal freedom between the stimulus and our response. How we choose to respond to something is our choice and can change our lives. Learning how to be healthily detached instead of being codependent is that personal freedom. It will put you back in charge of your business. I know many of the direct selling companies I work with and the clients I coach there have spouses who don't support their businesses and try to manage and control them out of doing it. Here is where you can start acting like a CEO and quit being codependent, letting them control you that way. The best way to get someone off your back is to *prove them wrong.* Get your shit together and start running a successful business—making money and feeling great about yourself. Guess what happens? They quit trying to manage you. So quit blaming them and start proving them wrong by getting serious about your business and implementing everything I am teaching you in this book. This is a huge concept that I am simply introducing you to. If this is resonating with you, I highly encourage you to pick up books by Melody Beattie. When I read her book, *Codependent No More,* many years ago, I was separated from my husband, and my therapist suggested I might be codependent. While I was quite offended (as most of my clients are when I suggest they might be as well), I was also intrigued and interested in doing anything it took to get healthy.

One Sunday morning, I started reading *Codependent No More,* and I couldn't put it down. At one point, I literally threw the book on the floor as if it was on fire and yelled aloud, alone in my apartment, "Oh my gosh! I HAVE THAT!" It was as if someone was writing about me and how I had been acting most of my life—I just didn't realize it was an actual thing. Well, it is. And learning about it, using it in my life every single day, and recovering from it has changed my life in so many ways, including how I run my business and how I can be in close relationship with so many clients and not take on their stuff.

I recently had a long-term client get rather aggressive with me. She was attacking the way I did my work. I will admit I was pissed at first. I then took some time to consider if I was doing something wrong, because I always ask myself if I own any part of criticism that comes my way. It took me about 48 hours to realize I didn't and that she was unhappy with her own life, feeling not especially loved by me, and instead of dealing with her own feelings, since that is much more uncomfortable, she decided to jump on my side of the net to attack and try to manage me. After taking about 48 hours to get myself straight, clear, and in a place of compassion for what I imagined she was feeling, we were able to discuss peacefully what was going on. I honor her ability to receive that information, and in fact, our working relationship has grown much stronger as a result.

I must warn you, this is not a quick process; it is a lifelong process. I call myself a recovering codependent, as I have frequent relapses of allowing others to manage and control me or wanting to jump in and fix something when it is none of my business. Having the awareness of who I am, my Type, and my form of codependency has brought so much calm into my life and given me so much more energy since I am not worrying about or managing things I don't need to be a part of. It is the most freeing feeling in the world! I want that for you too. Doing this work has allowed me to be exponentially more successful as an entrepreneur and coach. It isn't easy, but it is so worth it.

Almost all of us are codependent in one or more ways, because we have simply learned to be that way. However, we are uncomfortable looking at ourselves as being part of the problem. It is easier to blame other people than to look at yourself, but this book is about looking at yourself, learning who you are, and embracing the truth. You can do this!

Understanding Type and learning about codependency has

changed my life and so many of my clients' lives. I encourage you to start accepting who you innately are, living accordingly, and then start living a healthy, detached lifestyle.

Before we close this section I want to leave you with a few thoughts. Do what your heart is calling you to do and don't listen to naysayers. What the hell do they know anyway? We all have different paths, thank goodness. You have to starting living your life unapologetically as who you are. If you are meant to be in corporate America, then rock it, but if you are meant to march to the beat of your own drum and do your own thing, by all means do that! Sometimes we just have to leap! However, we also have to have a plan. You have to know where you are going and how you are going to get there. While I am a dreamer Intuitive Type, I am also a getter done'er Judger Type, and we must have both in order to be successful. If you are going to prove everyone else wrong, you need to have a plan, drive, ambition, and execution. No more excuses. Instead, take action with systems, structures, and singular focus!

We are now going to take everything you have learned about yourself in this section of *Who Are You?* and apply it to designing a magnificent life and successful business. Let's explore, *Where Are You Going?*

SECTION 3

Roadmap to
Where Are You Going?
Up-Leveling Your Mindset

CHAPTER 15

Up-Leveling Your Mindset

Now that we have determined who you are, it is time to figure out where you are going based on your personality Type and the things you are innately good at. Then you can start dreaming big. Your current mindset may very well be a huge part of what is holding you back in succeeding in your business, and it is a critical part of all success. It is time to up-level your mindset!

Mindset is critical to success because it has become proven, through quantum physics and quantum theory, that what we think about all day we become. Webster's definition of quantum theory is "a theory based on the concept of the subdivision of radiant energy into finite quanta and applied to numerous processes involving transference or transformation of energy into an atomic or molecular scale." Basically, your energy, thoughts, and feelings get transferred into your life. So this section is going to test a few of you as I am going to ask you to get honest about what you are putting into your heart, mind, and soul each day. What are you choosing to focus on? Likely, your current state of being in your life and business is an exact match to what you think about all day. We need to do some digging into what got you here, so let's start there.

This section, *Where Are You Going,* is going to be an honest assessment of:

- Where your current mindset is and how it got there.
- Where your mindset needs to be and why.
- How we can up-level it to change your life and business.

Your Current Mindset

"Maybe you have to let go of who you were to become who you will be."

—CARRIE BRADSHAW

Our current, limited mindset comes from our families, society, teachers, etc. We are bombarded with negativity on television and social media, which also plays a huge factor in how we currently think and feel. I am going to ask you to look deep during this section about how your past (family, teachers, stories that were told to you) and your present (what you are choosing to put into your body, mind, and soul) are affecting your current belief system about yourself and what you are capable of accomplishing in your business.

One of the first things we need to do before we move on to the manifesting phase is clean up some of your limiting beliefs and figure out how they got there.

Most of the beliefs you have are limiting beliefs. These beliefs are keeping you from Living Your Life from the Front Seat. They are keeping you from being abundant. They are keeping you from being yourself. They are keeping you from having love in your life. They are keeping you from joy and happiness. As we discover some of your current beliefs, you will likely find there were a few beliefs that don't quite mesh with who you want to be.

My limiting beliefs came around my worth as a human being and as a woman in dating relationships and in marriage. I came to believe I wasn't worth being faithful to, or the first priority, and it showed up in all kinds of yucky ways (like chasing the wrong men to validate myself). I told you I was a work in progress, right? I had to get clear about the difference between the beliefs that were given to me by others and what is actually true about myself—how God created me. And let me just say, that took time being alone, getting quiet, being ok dating myself, not needing or seeking validation from anyone other than myself, God, and those important in my life. No matter what your circumstances, doing that work will change your life and make you so much happier and calmer. I know it is extremely uncomfortable for most people to look at their shit and decide what they want to do with it, but I promise you this is an essential part of self-evolution or we just keep looking for something or someone else to validate us.

This is where I get my nickname Jessica "kick" Butts; we all need a good kick in the ass sometimes, and this is likely why you picked up this book! You have to be willing to dig deep and look at some of your old stuff as well as your current habits that keep you stuck. And this is an ongoing, never-ending process if you want to keep growing and evolving as a human being.

This is where so many people get and stay stuck. I am sure you have heard of the terms "victim" and "martyr." These types of people stay stuck in the past and can't see themselves in a new life. Victims think they cannot move forward because of their circumstances and often blame those circumstances and others for their problems. Martyrs complain and complain, but never do anything about it. It is a painful and sad thing to watch because there *is* a way out of it.

I hope how we acquired some of these limiting beliefs and small-minded mindsets is clear by now, but let's make all this crystal clear with an example of how others can affect us.

I recently heard through some friends that an acquaintance of mine was telling people that my success can't last and asking what I was going to do when people stopped paying me to help them and quit buying my books. I actually cackled out loud. Yes, I cackle! But I also realized how sad that was for *her*.

She is living a life of lack and scarcity and is sadly a complete victim to her circumstances that she created. She cannot see good for others because she is so stuck in her own messy life. I pray you are not one of those people, but you may very likely have some of those people in your life. If so, I urge you to distance yourself from them.

Don't you dare let their limiting beliefs and lack of mindset stop you.

Their stinkin' thinking has *nothing* to do with you anyway! Her comments have nothing to do with me, as she barely knows me or anything about my business. That is all her garbage that she projects onto other people. It is a sad reality that if someone is stuck in a bad relationship or job, they usually don't want to see others succeed because it makes them feel bad about themselves. This has nothing to do with you and you must get away from that. In the next section we are going to discuss the importance of the five people you spend the most time with. But for now, I would like you to list those five people and what you spend your time talking about: Do you gossip? Do you talk about silly reality TV shows (that aren't real)? Do you complain about your jobs? Complain about your spouses? Complain about being broke?

Or do you talk about how to grow your business? Do you talk about ideas? Do you talk about excellent personal development books? Do you share up-leveling podcasts? Do you lift each other up or tear each other down?

I actually want you to do this exercise right now since this is a HUGE part of what is being put into our mindsets. List the five people you spend the most time with and what you spend your time doing and talking about. I know this may not be easy, but as my former coach used to say, *how you do anything is how you do everything.* So, if you skip this exercise, what other hard things in your life are you skipping?

1. _____

_____

_____

_____

_____

2. _____

3. _____

4. _____

5. _____

In addition to these people in your life, some other ways the negative outside world can get into our mindset and start tainting it is:

- TV
- News
- Gossip
- Fear-based people
- Naysayers
- Our loving but old school parents who think being creative can't be a real job
- Communities we live in
- Corporate America, pensions holding people hostage

Please be aware of what is being placed into your mind every day by things and people around you. You get to choose what is going in by choosing who you hang out with, what television shows you watch, and the news you choose to listen to.

Your past, as well as your present life, hold so many false limiting beliefs; the first step to changing them is to become *aware*. To break through my limiting beliefs from childhood and my marriage (that I wasn't good or worthy enough), I had to become aware that those beliefs came from outside myself. God did not create me that way; others put that garbage onto me and I can choose to release what no longer serves me (and wasn't even true in the first place). I urge you to do this work so you can shake off what others have placed on you that no longer serves where you are going in this world. I believe you are ready to soar, but to soar you have to lighten your load.

Our pasts don't leave us; they most certainly stay with us. In fact, I believe wholeheartedly that they make up our uniqueness, specialness, and the reason we should be doing the work we are doing. As I have mentioned a few times already, your mess is your message. It is not about exploiting it, but it certainly is part of what makes you uniquely you (and likely how other people are going to connect with you). So stop thinking you have to be perfect to get clients. The oppression I felt in my marriage is absolutely part of why I do what I do and why my message resonates with the people it does. You are very likely the same. We acknowledge, release, and then use that mess as our message to do what we are passionate about.

It is not about airing your dirty laundry or ever using clients as a sounding board, but knowing that you have worked or are working through your shit is very refreshing and real. So are you ready to go on this journey of releasing what is no longer serving you so you can *dream*, *plan*, and *do* what you are meant to be doing in this world? You ready to jump? Let's go...

Roadmap to Your New Up-Leveled Mindset

"She believed she could, so she did."

—UNKNOWN

To do this fun, creative work you need to be in your Front Seat; you must be in a place of authenticity. You can only look forward when you are in your Front Seat. Let me say that again—you can only look forward and manifest your dreams when you are in your Front Seat. Our Back Seat is looking back. It is fearful, worried, and not in alignment with the Universe. Remember, it has the energy of a Drunk and a Baby, you do not want these parts of yourself running any part of your life. So, if you need to get into your Front Seat, please try to do so now by doing a few of the Front Seat activities I suggested in the last section. Take a break to dance, talk to a friend, cook, or exercise if you need to.

Now that you have done your Front Seat activities, here are some questions to ask yourself:

> What do you *want* in your life?
> How do you want to *feel*?
> How do you want to spend your *time*?
> *Who* do you want to spend your time with?
> What kind of *work* do you want to be doing?
> How do you want to *look* and *feel*?
> What kind of *environment* do you want to work in?

Now that you know who you are, your innate personality Type, unique abilities, what you suck at, and your codependent style, it's time to dive into what is likely keeping you stuck and things you may not want to look at (but must in order to grow and evolve). My coach recently said, "Your business grows proportionally to your personal development." I couldn't agree more. If you are not looking at some of the things I am about to introduce to you, along with understanding your innate personality type, there is no way to grow and evolve. I would venture to guess that nearly 100% of my clients, when they first come to me, are stuck here, spinning their wheels, trying and trying to do the "right" thing, and getting nowhere. If this is you, you are in luck; this section can and will change your life and business if you are willing to do the work.

What most people spend a lot of time doing is moving away from the thing they don't want in their life anymore, but they make the huge mistake of not figuring out where they want to go next. This is one of the #1 steps every successful business owner takes: you must see past today!

Business planning is critical. We are going to start by doing some big visioning, and then we will end with mapping it out, planning, and getting it done.

You must stop living five minutes in front of your face if you want to be successful! Most perceiving types (Ps) live like this, just getting by with the moment, but to be successful in businesses you must see and make a long-term plan. The last section of this book is about action; as no good planning, dreaming, envisioning, and manifesting is any good if you don't also take action. But for now let's focus on some key areas:

- Mindset
- Gratitude Journal
- Vison Boards
- Manifesting/Visualization
- Mind Maps

In this section, we're going to explore your thoughts, beliefs, mindset, and how you can up-level them to create the life of your dreams with a few simple, yet extremely effective, tools. Many of them you have likely heard of before, some you haven't. Either way, I want you to come at them with a new attitude and fresh new perspective.

These are truly life changing tools, and now that you know yourself much better, it is time to do them from that new vantage point. Got it? OK, let's go.

Mindset

You've probably heard a lot lately about this thing called "mindset" or the "law of attraction." The most basic way I can break it down is this:

We are what we think about all day.
What we think about all day, we become.
What we think about expands.

That is really all there is to it. If you are thinking about negative things, if you are thinking about where you could be, or where you should (#banishshould) be, or focusing on the thing you are trying to back away from, you are never going to get to where you need to be. Ever. You need a mind shift change!

When I first finished graduate school and started my private practice, I had no clients and didn't exactly know how to get them, either. I woke up every morning and went to the other room and did 22 minutes of guided life visualization meditation. I needed to dream it and see it so I could plan it. If I didn't have visions of a full practice, speaking on large stages, and sharing my gifts, I would not have known what to do in the next 24 hours. You must have a long-term vision for your life so you know what you are working toward. The good news is God does not give you all the visions at the same time—or you would go nuts! He drips them out to you as you proceed on your journey. So whatever He is giving you now will grow and evolve as you grow and evolve in your business.

I had visions of speaking on large stages in those mornings all those years ago. I had no idea how I was going to get there, but having that strong vision each day paved the way for my books, coaching programs, and speaking career. If you don't believe me, try it!

Have you ever wanted to move on from an experience that was negative and end up finding yourself in a similar situation a little later in life? Many people do just that, and they end up repeating history rather than moving on. Why? This happens because they are often looking back rather than looking forward.

If you want to move forward, you can't be looking back all the time to see where you are in relation to where you came from. If we're going to use the driving metaphor again, it's hard to go forward and get to your destination if you are only looking out your rearview mirror. You're going to crash into something, and chances are it's going to lo ok a lot like the wreck you left behind.

You need to turn away from that past and focus firmly on what's next. You have to leave that wreck in the rearview mirror behind, and look at the road in front of you. Be aware of your surroundings and what's going on around you so you can navigate confidently to your destination.

What are those wrecks you're leaving behind you? They're your traumas and your failed relationships. They're false beliefs about yourself given to you by someone else. They may simply be where you once were but you have evolved past. If you continue to focus on your past, you become a victim of your history. I'm calling you out and telling you this backwards thinking has to stop. You can't keep focusing on what you don't want if you want to move forward. You have to turn away from it and focus on something you truly want. If you continue to focus on what you don't want, you end up attracting the thing you least desire. I believe this is where almost everyone gets stuck.

My coach calls this behavior "chaotic energy", but I prefer to call it "wonky energy." If you've ever dealt with a two-year-old, you know they don't understand the word "don't." Your subconscious mind and the Universe are a lot like a two-year-old child. If you say, "I don't want to be broke," your subconscious mind and the Universe don't hear the word "don't;" they just hear "broke" and help you get there. Saying, "I don't want to be broke" doesn't make sense to the Universe. The Universe does not know what that energy means. All it hears is "broke." You might say or express "I don't want to be in this bad relationship anymore." But what the Universe hears is "bad relationship." I also have a funny saying about God: "He is busy so we need to be specific with our prayers." God doesn't exactly know what "I want to be happy" means. It is our job to get specific about what we are commanding of the Universe and praying to God for. Do your job, get clear on what you want to ask for, and it can happen much more quickly and easily.

So your work is going to be deciding exactly what you want

in your life in the next 90 days, one year, five years, and beyond. What will you focus on? How are you going to focus your energy and attention to a positive place? By turning toward, and focusing on, the life you are designing for yourself.

I recently had a client who kept saying she wanted to grow her business, but the more she spoke, she kept contradicting herself by saying things like, "I really enjoy spending time with my toddler right now and I'm not sure how much I want to work during this phase of his life." I fully believe in spending time with your family and growing your business, and there is no judgment either way, but we must be clear about our intentions so they are in alignment. If you want to spend time with your children over the summer or during a phase in their lives, that's fantastic, but be clear why your business isn't growing.

I created a boot camp a few years ago that didn't quite feel right. I worked really hard to make it a success, but deep down I knew it wasn't the work I was supposed to be doing. So, while I asked and asked for the Universe to bring me clients for it, I didn't believe because I couldn't visualize doing that work long-term. It was chaotic/wonky energy.

The lesson is this: if you are asking for something and it is not coming, you need to check with yourself to make sure it is what you really want, that your energy is in alignment, and that you really believe it. We are co-creators of our experience, and our world, with the Universe and God. It is a team effort and we must be in alignment with our team!

For just a moment, try this exercise: In the room where you are now, imagine the thing you are trying to move on from in one corner of the room. This can be anything: a bad relationship, a death, or anger towards someone. Now step back, but stay focused on it.

Can you see anything else? Probably not. All your attention and focus are on the thing you don't want in your life.

Slowly turn around and imagine, in the other corner of the

room, the things you do want: love, freedom, fun, a career you love, abundance of ideal clients, travel, friends, or fulfillment—whatever you truly want for yourself. You must shift your mental focus to the new in order for it to come to you. To succeed and reach your goals, you must *turn* towards the thing you want to *go* towards.

I have learned through the years that as much as we can manifest by doing all these activities, we don't determine when the result comes to us; God does. God is in charge of when he brings our dreams to us. Our job is to keep believing.

Before we move on, I want to give you a couple of examples of things in my life I believed would happen, not just things I hoped would happen.

- I KNEW I would have a successful and full private practice. I knew it, I believed it, and therefore I took every action necessary to make that happen. I saw it before it was even a reality.
- I have also visualized places I would live far before I moved there. I imagined the color of the walls, the things that would surround me, where it was in the Seattle area. I have lived a couple of places that I have visualized before I even knew they existed.
- I have visualized the relationship of my dreams, I see it, therefore there is no settling until it arrives.

I also do this exercise with almost every important day in my life. I create it in my mind before the event happens. When I speak, I see the room where I will be speaking. I see the crowd responding to me. I play out in my mind how I do, how I feel, what I say. It is not rehearsed word for word, but rather I see how the entire thing plays out.

In short, our mind doesn't know the difference between our imagination and reality. You have the power to create the reality you want rather than what you have always had before!

So how do you do this? And what does it have to do with type? Well, to start with, as we already know, Intuitive people are natural dreamers. They're always imagining "what if," both for good and ill. Sensing Types are more likely to live in the moment and not spend time imagining or dreaming about what they truly want or desire.

But this is where I ask you to both make a commitment to shift your reality by learning and doing daily visualization exercises. Sensors will typically say "show me" and ask for proof, but I'm going to challenge you to suspend disbelief in this sort of thing and just trust me that it works, because it most certainly does. It only takes you a few minutes each day to work on your visualizations to create the life of your dreams. Plus, it's fun and you will thank me!

The Vortex and the Front Seat

"As you think, you vibrate. So what you are thinking and what is coming back to you is always a vibrational match."

—ABRAHAM HICKS

Before you begin the mindset work, it's important for you to first get into your Front Seat as we talked about in the last section. This is the first time we are going to put your Front Seat activities into use.

Abraham-Hicks coined a phrase about "getting into the Vortex" in their book, *Ask and it is Given.* The Vortex is the equivalent of being in the Front Seat, which is all about being in alignment with your best self and the Universe. When you are in your Front Seat, you are in a place of believing and authenticity. Being in your Front Seat gets you into the Vortex—doing things that make you happy, bringing energy, and renewing your soul.

But if you've been living from the Back Seat for a while, it might be tough to get into your physical/emotional/spiritual Front Seat. One of the best ways to do that is to do something you enjoy. This is the time to practice those activities. Here is a short reminder of some activities based on your type:

Extroverts:	Being with people
	Talking with a friend
	Dancing
Introverts:	Cooking alone
	Journaling
	Reading
	Deep conversation with a great friend
Intuitives:	Being creative
	White space to just imagine
Sensing:	Making a list
	Doing something with your hands
NP:	Starting a new fun project
SP:	Being active with hands or body
NJ:	Creating something new
SJ:	Taking care of something

The Vortex and being in your Front Seat are all about doing things that make you feel good and get you into your rhythm and best space. For me as an ENFJ, I like to listen and dance to music that gets me in a good mood, allow white space for creativity, check things off my to do list, have a deep conversation with a friend, or take a walk in nature.

What are your Front Seat activities again? Have you thought of any more? List them here:

_____

_____

_____

_____

_____

Now that you have a list of a few things, do them! The next chapter is going to be all about action, and these are part of your new normal—things you do every day to get you to be your best self. You must, must, MUST do these, ideally every day, but at least four to five times a week. Notice your energy shift. You will be amazed.

Gratitude Journal

*"Appreciation in advance
brings everything you want to you."*

—ABRAHAM HICKS

A gratitude journal is different from a free-write journal, because it is specifically for listing all the things you are grateful for. *The Five-Minute Journal* is an excellent example of a starter journal that also helps you focus on the things you are grateful for.

Anytime we focus on the positive of anything or anyone, that which we are focused on grows. If you have watched or read *The Secret* (and if you haven't, you should) you know they spend an entire chapter preaching this same message.

What you are feeling and focusing on in any given moment will create the next moment (and the next and the next), so if in this moment you are grateful for your partner, your bank account, your health, your clients, and your business, that vibrational energy and good feeling will carry on to the next moment, eventually creating a virtual lifetime of seeing the good in most situations. And feeling good creates good. As long as you are also taking consistent action, you can't help but create gratitude and abundance in your life, and who doesn't want that? It really takes three things to be successful 1) understanding your innate personality Type 2) up-leveling your mindset 3) taking action.

You know people who always have something going wrong, don't you? They are creating their yucky life themselves. Let's get real. Bad stuff happens to everyone, but when you change the way you see it and deal with it, you will notice a difference. Speaking ill will or complaining all day about your job will only create more misery for yourself and, trust me, your friends and family are also really sick of it!

A great example of this is for those of you who still have a 9-5 job and want to quit and start your own business. I ask my clients in this situation to try to see their current job not as a death sentence, but as a means to help them create this new business. Starting a business is hard work and quite expensive. Most everyone needs a coach (don't reinvent the wheel, people; hire someone who has an excellent track record to help you), website, branding, marketing strategy, list generation, package pricing, or some other help. You can choose to see your current job as horrific, which it might very well be, or you can see it as your cash cow to help you launch your business. It can, and likely will, completely change the way to see it.

This perspective becomes your own little secret and can help you be grateful for your situation instead of despise it. I encourage you to spend some time each morning and throughout the day being grateful for the things and people in your life instead of nitpicking all the bad. You will be amazed how your life magically gets better just by choosing to be grateful!

Here is a sample list:

> I am grateful for: My career, God answering prayers, fun dinners with my sister, deep connections with close friends, my beautiful home, my soft sheets, my wonderful partner, fresh flowers, game night and dinner with friends, watermelon water, ETSY, the upcoming Seahawks season, cold brew coffee at Starbucks, living in beautiful Seattle, rainy Sunday mornings, sunshine on my face, taking walks in middle of the day, kisses, cuddling on the couch, the beach, Maui, Cabo, Italy, pink lip gloss, hair color, happy hour, laptops.

You get the idea. Instead of complaining, be grateful. Every day.

Visualization

*"Change your thoughts and
you'll change your world."*

—UNKNOWN

How do you get clear on what you want? One of the tools I have used throughout my life to help me accomplish what I wanted has been visualization. It is also where you need to start.

Visualization is using imagination to create a picture of what your desired outcome will be. If you want to be successful, how does that look to you? How is your physical health? How are your relationships? Where is your house? What kinds of vacations are you taking? How often do you work? What kind of work are you doing? When you can create a visual picture in your mind of the life you want to lead, you are already helping the Universe (or God) to help you get where you want to go.

Our brain and subconscious do not know the difference between imagined and real. So by visualizing, you are tricking yourself, brain, and the Universe into believing it is already happening. You have the feelings associated with already having the thing you want in your life. For example, if you want a wonderful, loving relationship, imagine having it every day. Feel what it feels like to have that relationship, imagine yourself together with your partner, the things you do together, how you look at each other, where you go, how you have sex, and how you make each other feel. Imagine it all as if it is happening!

I did this every single day for about a year, and still do at least a couple of times a week, to visualize what my business would look like and how I would feel doing it. Imagine your business at its peak level, making money, fulfilled, helping people, organized. Who is on your team? What do your days look like? Where do you see your business in five years? How are you best expressing yourself through authentic marketing? See these things for your business and the day to day work will start to align to help you get there.

Some people might call it daydreaming, but it's really just creating that picture—that feeling—of what you're going to do. I did this a lot when I played softball in high school. I would imagine myself running and catching the ball and throwing it and making a great play. I would do it over and over in my head, and I know that it helped me be a stronger ball player.

As I mentioned earlier, I do this when I speak as well. I do this when I need to have a difficult conversation or do anything that I really want in order to trick my mind and subconscious into believing it has already happened the way I want it to happen. And it seriously works!

The crazy part about all of this is you have control over your own life because you have control over your own thoughts. For some of you that is good news, and for some that is a very scary thought. Either way, it is 100% true. So what do you want to do—create a crappy life or create an awesome one?

Even pro athletes do this. Recently, I read that the world champion

Seahawks quarterback, Russell Wilson, does the same sort of thing. Before the game, Russell goes down onto the field and visualizes his game for the day. He sees the play, the ball, how he throws, everything. Olympic athletes do this. Skaters, skiers, swimmers, wrestlers, lifters, runners—they all do it. They visualize their performance first and then they do it.

Back when I was working in corporate America over ten years ago, I knew I was going to have an office with my own private practice. That was despite all the naysayers who told me I was crazy to dream this dream. My ex-husband told me I was crazy. My colleagues in corporate America told me I was nuts. But every night, before I drove home, I could see there were therapists' offices in my office building. I said, "That's where my office is going to be." When I graduated, I went back to that building and lo and behold, there was an office for rent. I walked in and told the management, "I don't even care how much this costs, this is where I am supposed to be. I'll take it." People in the industry (psychotherapy) told me there was no way I was going to be able to build my practice to a profitable place within three years, but I knew I could. I had seen it already happen in my mind. I achieved my goal in less than half that time; in just a year and a half I had a full practice.

Now, those same people who were my naysayers are coming to me and asking me how I did it. How I got the office I wanted, where I wanted, with the work that I wanted to do. It all comes down to my mindset. I just knew it. I visualized it, I saw it, and I believed it. I also worked my butt off, as simply visualizing, seeing, and believing isn't enough. I had to put my belief into action (which is the final part of this book).

I also have a not-so-positive example, but one that is just as powerful, and I hope it helps you think about the positive and negative mindset beliefs you may already have. I didn't realize when I got married that I had a belief it wouldn't last forever. That was not a conscious thought, but a subconscious belief based on my family, as they were all divorced. This was pointed out to me years later in therapy with my ex-husband. It was a huge wake-up call for me about the power of our subconscious beliefs.

All of these tools are amazing, but being able to visualize is at the core of all of them. This technique is going to be easier for Intuitive Types because our brains are already designed to do this, but Sensors can certainly do this as well.

Judgers will likely want to do all of these right away. If you can do that, great, but you may also want to do one or two immediately and add the rest in later. The Perceivers are likely to be excited about trying them all, but may not follow through on any of them, so I encourage you to do these with a friend and hold yourself accountable to start incorporating these techniques into your daily life.

So what do you need to do? It is quite simple, really. You simply close your eyes and see it already happening. It can take one minute, two hours, or longer. Start to visualize the things you really want in your life with the following exercises I am about to teach you.

Vision Boards

"If you can dream it, you can do it"

—WALT DISNEY

One of my all-time favorite exercises is using a vision board!

Everyone should have a vision board, but especially entrepreneurs and business owners as we must have a vision for our business and our ideal clients. One of the sayings I cut out and put on my vision board years ago when I was still doing therapy full time was, "Developing High Performing Women Every Day." I wasn't necessarily doing that back then, but it is currently 100% of my business, and I wouldn't have it any other way.

All Types will benefit from this exercise and will likely go about it differently, so let me explain this before we go on.

Intuitive Types love this because it is visual and creative. This will likely be one of your favorite exercises. If you have done it before, great, but do a new one now. In fact, update it constantly. The visual component of this exercise is something you should be updating at least every six months.

Sensing Types love the tactile creativity of the exercise. You will enjoy cutting out the pictures, figuring out where to put them, and how to arrange them. Where the Sensing Types may prefer the specifics and details of the goal cards, this is also an incredibly important exercise to push your big picture thinking.

NPs, as always, will have difficulty finishing the project, but you still need to; find a friend to do it with and make a pact you will finish it together.

NJs will need to try not to micromanage the project and allow for their creativity to be alive.

SJs will need to allow for the creativity of the project to flow and stop the thinking that it is silly. It will open up a new part of your mind, literally.

SPs will want to just play with the pictures and may not want to finish it. Just finish it already!

Vision boards allow you to play with pictures and words that create a certain feeling. The vision board is, in essence, a visual of the things you want in your life.

The vision board is a daily visual reminder of where you are going and how you want to feel. You can use whatever medium you want to make this vision board. Some people cut up old magazines, others find pictures on Pinterest or Google Images and then print them out.

You might think you need to make a vision board intentionally, looking for specific pictures or images. You can, however, simply allow yourself to feel drawn to images and words and put them together on your vision board.

As a rule, I recommend making a vision board at least once a year, but twice a year is better. I know some people who make a new vision board every quarter (or at least update it quarterly). The great thing about vision boards is that the things will start to come true and you can replace them with new, bigger visions.

Since writing *Live Your Life from the Front Seat* I have come to realize there is one specific place in your home that is perfect for your vision board: your bathroom! I have since moved my vision board to my bathroom wall and mirror since the point of your vision board is to see it as much as possible so it gets into your subconscious. I never realized how much idle time I have in the bathroom while I am brushing my teeth, washing my face, getting ready in the morning, and even pooping. I now feel even more productive during that time when I am getting ready in the morning and getting ready for bed at night because I know I am actively engaging my subconscious with what I most desire in life.

Many years ago, I took a hypnotherapy certification course and while I didn't end up practicing the work I did learn a great deal about the power of our subconscious. What we think about all day (also what we look at all day) we create. You want to spend as much time as possible looking at the things you desire in life, so be specific about what is on your vision board. For business owners, it should be happy clients, piles of money, speaking, memes, and words to describe how you want your business.

If you are just starting out on a vision board and don't know what you want yet, you can scroll through magazines or Pinterest and just let images that strike you pop forward and then cut them out. When I went through my divorce and felt a little lost and didn't know what I needed at the time, the theme for my vision board turned out to be powerful, luminous women. I didn't realize it when I chose the pictures; I simply allowed myself to choose pictures that resonated or spoke to me at the time and cut them out. Once I was going through them I realized I had a theme—I imagine you will have a similar experience. I then noticed that I started feeling lighter and freer and happier. Shortly afterwards, I started to lose the weight that I had been struggling to get rid of. I felt lighter, and I knew that a part of it is because I saw those images in my vision board every single day. It's just like Wallace Wattles says, "The impressing of these images on the mind every day makes an impact on the mind."

I promise you that having a vision board will help you manifest what it is that you want in your dream life. Dream big and remember that not everyone wants the same thing, so don't judge what is on yours. I have many Maui houses that are currently out of reach, but I believe wholeheartedly that continuing to work hard, leveraging my business, doing what I love, being in alignment with what's important to me, and manifesting it through goal cards, vision boards, and visualization will make it happen. Follow me on Instagram (Front Seat Life) to find out *when* it happens.

Goal Cards

"Don't be afraid to give yourself everything you've ever wanted in life!"

—UNKNOWN (SOMEONE AWESOME)

As an Intuitive Type, I am an intensely visual person. I have always been able to create my own pictures in my head—to visualize the things that I wanted. Because of this, it has always just come naturally to me to do visualization, and see myself doing what I wanted to be doing. But when I learned about and started using goal cards in September of 2013, my successes exploded exponentially!

So what is a goal card? It is a card or anything else you choose to write on with your manifestations written out so you can read it every single day. I use mine as book marks for my morning practice, so each morning I open my journal or daily read book there are my goal cards.

A goal card is your vision board or visualization in written form, written as if you already have it using language that is:

- Specific
- Positive
- Present Tense (as if you already have it)

Then read your goal cards every single day. This daily practice powerfully reinforces your visualizations.

Here's an example that an aspiring marathon runner might use:

> "I am at the Boston Marathon. I feel full of energy, my body is healthy and strong, my mind is clear and I am running my best time ever, placing me in the top twenty."

Another example of a goal card could read:

> "I am working in the career of my dreams. I easily and effortlessly find the perfect new job. I am happy, fulfilled, and making great money. I come home to my family at the end of the day full of love and energy."

A goal card can contain anything you want. It can be a sticky note. It can be a file card. The key to making a goal card is that you write down exactly what you want and then look at the card every day, reading the card aloud often. It doesn't have to be fancy, but if you're like me, a bit of sparkle and prettying up helps me to have even better thoughts and feelings about those goals that I have expressed. So if flowers make you feel happy, feel free to decorate your goal cards with flowers. If sparkle makes you feel happy, decorate it with sparkly things. If cars or planes or exotic locations make you feel happy, use those too. You can make it as simple or as loud as you want—it's your goal! Once it is written, you need to read it aloud as often as possible. My friend Kris taught me that reading things aloud is better than reading them to yourself (although that is also helpful), because our throat chakra is our manifestation center. So it helps to read it aloud in order to believe it.

I use my goal cards as bookmarks for daily practice books so I am sure to read them every morning as part of my morning routine. However, you might have yours on the bathroom mirror, beside your computer monitor, on a special board or even in the kitchen on your refrigerator.

So far, I've been talking about just one card. But the truth of the matter is, you can have as many goal cards as you like and need. Your goals don't all happen at the same time. They don't all manifest right away. So using goal cards to help you focus on the next goal *and* the other goals that are going to help you accomplish magnificent things just makes sense. Make as many as you want to make, but make them as if you already have that thing you desire.

I'm going to share with you some of the goal cards I made just last year. Some of these goals have already come into being, and others have not yet.

When I was writing a goal card for this book, I wrote "My book is magnificent, beautiful, and successful. It is better than I can even imagine. People can't wait to buy it. It is completely and easily done within a year. People are drawn to it. I can't wait to share it and it provides me so many opportunities."

One about my weight (wow, I am getting really vulnerable

sharing my actual goal cards and size here, but it is all in service to you!) reads, "I am a perfect size 10, healthy and happy. I feel sexy, confident, and great in and out of my clothes."

When I was seeking new ideal clients I wrote, "My energy and light attract my ideal clients." When I realized I was putting too much effort into it, and not allowing enough, I wrote, "I am open to receiving the gifts from God and the Universe. My life is easy, calm, exciting, happy, fulfilled, and abundant."

What are you noticing about my goals? They are positive, in the here and the now, and done easily. Some may be long, but some can be only a few words.

A few years ago I realized I had a belief that life needed to be hard so I felt like I really earned things (although I have always worked extremely hard), and that belief put obstacles in my way. I decided I didn't need or want that limited belief in my life anymore, so I wrote a goal card that simply said, "My life is easy." Since that day my life has honestly become easier. I read it every day and believe it can be—so it is.

Now it is time for you to write some of your own goal cards. Use the space below to practice a few. Start with a few: one for your life, one for your relationships, and one for your career. Then get some cards, my goal cards or whatever you choose, to start using as part of your daily routine. I suggest having at least one for personal and one for your business because if we aren't taking care of ourselves we can't run an effective business long-term.

Personal:
_____
_____
_____
_____
_____

Business:

_____

_____

_____

_____

_____

Mind Mapping

"If you don't make the time to work on creating the life you want, you're eventually going to be forced to spend a LOT of time dealing with a life you don't want."

—KEVIN NGO

Mind mapping is essential for Intuitive Types because we are big picture dreamers and need a way to set goals that works for our type.

The SMART goal-setting system attributed to Peter Drucker is a great tool for Sensing Types to use. But you Intuitive Types may have felt constrained or restricted using this tool; I know I did. Peter uses SMART to represent goals that are Specific, Measurable, Achievable (although I say dream big), Relevant, and Time-bound. Sensing Types love these metrics. Intuitive Types need a little more wiggle room, but something just as powerful. Whatever your type, Sensing or Intuitive, you must try mind mapping.

Mind mapping is critically important and should be done quarterly. Once you have done the work of creating your vision board, and spent some time visualizing where you want your business to grow, the next step is getting those ideas out of your head and onto a mind map. You can do one for yourself and for your business if you would like. You can use the simple diagram below to get a visual of what I am teaching you, but you can google "mind maps" and literally thousands of ideas will show up to help you create your masterpiece. Or you can just keep it simple like I do.

The first step is to place your business in the middle circle; mine would read Front Seat Life. I am going to list them for ease of reading, but it may be too linear for Intuitive Types. Find the biggest piece of paper you can and "map" this out, do not simply list your goals. Our Intuitive brains work better with the large visual versus the list I am about to make for you but you can simply transfer the idea onto the mind map.

The arms of the circle are all the areas of your business that you need to focus on. Here's an example:

Social media

Instagram
» Instragram stories

FB
» Personal page
» Business page
» Private VIP pages
» 80% content-20% selling

Marketing
» Print material
» Events
» Networking
» Once a week getting out to meet people
» Zoom meetings

Clients

Loving on them
» Client appreciation gifts

Free get acquainted calls
» Timetrade set up for 15 min calls

Direct Selling Parties
» Three a month
» Reaching out to 20 people to get three

Website
» Keeping blog updated
» May need to update

This is just an example, but I hope you are getting the idea that there is always a lot to do in running your own business and we must get it out of our heads and have a plan. By the way, this might be a good time to invite you to my Front Seat Life Membership Group where I teach you how to do all these things. At my website **www.jessicabutts.com**, you can find out more and get yourself enrolled so you can run your business from the Front Seat. I don't want to leave you hanging as I want greatness for you, I can help.

Again, the idea behind all of the things I am teaching you in this section about up-leveling your mindset is this: if you don't have a plan of where you are going in your business you will never get anywhere. You must, must, must have a vision and a plan. Dream big and then work your ass off to get there. I am going to show you how to get there in Section 4, *Taking Action*.

How to Change Your Mindset

"Go confidently in the direction of your dreams.

Live the life you have imagined."

—HENRY DAVID THOREAU

By exploring your beliefs now, you are free to choose whether or not you want to continue to believe those things now. That's right. You are now free to choose whether you want to keep doing what you have done before; whether you want to keep believing the things that have made you play small and not Live Your Life from the Front Seat.

I mentioned Victor Frankel earlier and I want to highlight him again because his book *Man's Search for Meaning* is so powerful. He describes personal freedom as the place between the stimulus and our response.

Think about that for a moment. We are always triggered by some stimulus, there will always be a stimulus, always, and we have no control over that. None. That stimulus can be your boss being a jerk, the person that cut you off while driving to work, the rude clerk at the grocery store, or that difficult client. Whatever it is, you cannot control it, so why waste your limited precious energy trying to? What you do have control over is your response to that stimulus. That is personal freedom my friends.

The important thing about your mindset and what you put into it (whether it's visualization, vision boards, and goal cards), is that you need to have faith these goals will come to pass. Some might say you need to suspend disbelief, but I firmly believe you need to simply *believe*. Without a firm belief in your goal and that it will be, you'll end up looking backward instead of looking forward. Through belief and intention, you let the Universe fulfill your goal with grace and beauty in each moment. It's the feeling and knowledge that whatever you truly desire is already on its way to you, and so it is.

At first you might feel this is ridiculous and woo-woo. However, simply let go of those notions that hold you back from belief. In fact, I have had some coaches say, "Fake it 'til you make it." Pretend to believe until you can and do believe. Soon, when these goals start to come true, you will be able to simply trust that it is true, to "Let go and let God."

Remember to be patient with yourself and to give yourself (and the Universe) time to bring those changes into reality. It's all about the journey, not just the destination. Use your goal cards and vision board to help you begin your day with intention. Take time to meditate to better understand yourself and get greater clarity. Surround yourself with people who really understand you and who will support you when you need supporting.

In the next chapter, we will explore how you're going to get to your optimal destination. Then we'll bring all this back together so you can create an actionable plan to help you start Living Your Life from the Front Seat!

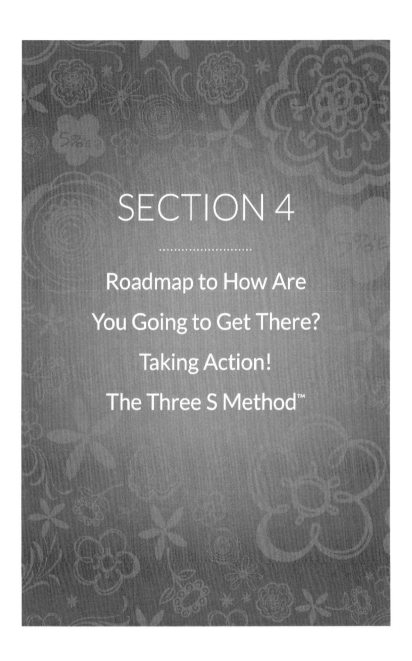

SECTION 4

Roadmap to How Are You Going to Get There?

Taking Action!

The Three S Method™

CHAPTER 16

Taking Action

Most things in life are meaningless without taking action. The popular saying is quite true, "Actions speak louder than words." When I was seeing clients as a couples' therapist, *taking action* was the number one attribute each person in the relationship wanted to see in the other. Words are meaningless when there is no action involved.

Think about that for a moment. Imagine someone in your life that has made empty promises to you. They were empty because there was no action to back up the promises. How did you feel? I bet you felt disappointed, annoyed, sad, let down, and lost. Please realize that you are doing the same thing to others, and more importantly to yourself, when you don't keep your word by taking consistent action.

How others feel is only one part of not taking action. The biggest, and most important, part is that there is no way your dreams for your business and your life can come true without taking the steps I am going to outline for you. I have compiled what I know to be the most valuable tools available to keep you focused and taking consistent action toward your goals and dreams.

Before we move on in this powerful section I need you to get honest with yourself about where you are choosing inaction in your life. I know this is hard to look at because it is easier to blame other people or circumstances, but it is truly on you if you are still stuck and not making progress. I have been there, just like all of you. Mine was more personal than in my business but since I am an entrepreneur, they are connected. I was stuck in my marriage for a long, long time. I used to blame him for me being stuck, but I have come to learn through years of therapy, coaching, and personal work that I was as much a part of our dysfunction as he was, mostly because I allowed it. I stayed and let our marriage hold me back. I spent years blaming him, crying on the kitchen floor, and letting his treatment of me define who I was. I told myself that if he could cheat on me I must be not worthy of anything, especially love.

In all honesty, it took years of taking action—not simply talking about it—to get out of that cycle. I also had to be away from that relationship to learn who I really am and what my talents and gifts are. I think back now on the difficult times of choosing to leave my marriage with nothing (worried I couldn't pay my own rent at 40 years old), and build a life I was meant to live. It was terrifying, and at times it still is, but if I had not chosen to take those actions, one step at a time, then I can say with all my heart I would not be here today writing this book.

I had a dream! That dream could not be fulfilled in the dysfunction of my marriage so I had to take action. I am not saying you have to do the same. In fact I hope you don't, as I love marriage and believe you can have an amazing business that fits with your personality and allows you to live your core values daily. There were a number of things wrong with my marriage that made it not work, but my part in that was to acknowledge *who I was*, have a *clear vision* for my life, and then take *action* to get myself there. We only get one life on this earth and I am hell-bent on making it the best one possible. If that involves leaving people who cannot fully support and love me, then that is what I have to do. What about you?

Actions without direction are pointless. We must make sure the decisions and actions we are taking are in alignment with who we are and what our mission is. The sequence of this book is intentional. I cannot start the book with taking action if you don't know who you are or what you want yet in life and your business. The steps below helped me in my decision making toward taking action and have helped thousands of my clients do the same.

Stuck Sucks!

There are no "wrong" decisions. A decision is a decision; it is not right or wrong. We have no idea what the future holds, so we can play out each scenario over and over until we have analysis paralysis and then we make no decision and we stay stuck. Stuck is the worst! I think of stuck as purgatory, a place between heaven and hell. That is no way to live your life. Take the time to figure out what you want and how you want to feel. Then make a damn decision. My guess is you will feel amazing once you have.

Sit with it. Sometimes you just need to leap and other times you need to take time to journal, talk to friends, get away, check in with your gut, talk to a therapist, or ask your coach. But then you must make a decision.

Head, heart, body. When I was going through my divorce I realized my head and my heart were both failing me. My head was being too "thinky" and my heart was too hurt to make a rational decision. They were in constant battle with one another and therefore not helping me at all. I discovered that a third tool to help me make a decision was my body. I would have a somatic response every time my ex-husband walked in the door or I thought about seeing him. My gut would clench and my body reacted like an opposite magnet to him. My body was telling me exactly what I needed. So listen to yours as well, because your body is likely telling you exactly what you need to know.

Small steps. Be clear that the first decision is likely not the only one you will need to make. However, once you are firm in your decision, I encourage you to stay strong and keep moving in that direction. My choice to not get a "real job" and pursue my private practice is a great example of that in my life. I made a choice and I did whatever it took to make my private practice work. I took small, consistent actions towards that goal every single day for 18 months. I got up early. I read every book I could get my hands on. I hired a coach I couldn't afford. I didn't go back to my husband, even though that was safe and easy. I rented an office I couldn't afford. I worked on the weekends and I saw clients late into the evening. Daily I took consistent and actionable steps towards my dream. I had a vision, knew what I wanted, and didn't let anything or anyone get in my way. You can absolutely do the same!

Butt tap. One of the coolest ways that God and the Universe speak to us is through what I like to think of as the "butt tap." Maybe you've had that experience when you've made a hard decision and start moving towards a dream and everything in your life starts to align. I think that is God giving you a loving butt tap letting you know that you are moving in the right direction. He has designed all of us to do something specific in this world; hence, all our different personality types. So, when He starts seeing us going in the right direction, he rewards us by lining up things on our behalf. It might look like getting your first client, finding the perfect assistant, or landing that great office. Not everything is going to be perfect, trust me, but I swear to you once you are on the right path you will feel God and the Universe's support behind you like a little tap on the butt.

Evolve. Lastly, evolve. We are all changing every single day. New experiences and people in our lives change who we are. You are not the same person you were five years ago, so give yourself some credit that you are growing and evolving. You may have been terrified to do something years ago, but I assure you that if you are reading great books, growing in your life and business, pushing yourself, and getting coached, then you are not the same person you were even yesterday. Evolving is what we humans are supposed to do.

Stop Lying to Yourself

Action backs up your convictions, your promises, your word, and your dreams. Intuitive Types love to dream, some of us in our heads and some of us extrovertedly by telling others. Unless we take action, it is only lip service and we begin to lose credibility with others and, more importantly, with ourselves.

Getting up every day and lying to yourself is a pretty sad way to start the day. Stop lying to yourself by saying you are going to do something and then not do it! Those lies may be about exercising, writing, working on your business, marketing, being loving to your partner, saving money, or getting on a budget. Whatever you need to work on, choose to do it once and for all. Be honest with yourself that you may not be able to do everything. I have made a *choice* to spend more time working on running and growing my business than on my physical fitness. That doesn't mean I don't do anything, but my precious morning time has to be focused time and I choose to spend that time on my business. So a few years ago I decided to quit lying to myself that I was going to get up and go to the gym. I felt so much better knowing that I am sticking to my word by getting up early to work on my spiritual health and my amazing business. Continuing to lie to yourself about something makes you feel like crap, which creates negative thinking. Remember, what we think about all day we become. If you think you are a lazy liar, that is going to grow, which is not good! So make a choice and take action toward your goal. Momentum will grow and you'll feel good, which in turn fuels positive thoughts.

Remember, what you are doing and thinking right now is affecting the next moment and the next, and the next. Be careful about what you are thinking.

Js and Ps

This is a good place to remind you that this section is going to be more difficult for Perceivers. Js are innately designed to take action and Ps are going to work harder on this section. I highly recommend that everyone get an accountability partner. I suggest that Ps partner up with a J and Js partner up with a P. Js will help Ps stay on task and Ps will remind Js that they need to enjoy some down time. As entrepreneurs, the job is never done, so we Js need a reminder from Ps that it is OK to play, take time off, and just be.

Here's a little tough love. If you are only talking about the things you want to accomplish in your life and business and are taking no action, then you are being a martyr. The definition of a martyr is someone who continues to complain about something and does nothing to fix it. Ouch! If this is you, are you ready to stop staying stuck and make some changes? I really hope so.

There is also the victim, someone who blames everyone else for the reason they can't accomplish things. They say, "I'm too tired, I have children, and I can't get up earlier…" I know plenty of amazing, successful people who have accomplished truly amazing things in their businesses all while raising children and dealing with life crises. When our dreams become non-negotiable, we will do anything to accomplish them. Anything. One of my clients right now is finishing her book and she has decided she will not watch

TV until her book is finished. I have chosen to get up an hour earlier, before 5 am, every single day for a month to finish the final edits of this book in order to get it done. I have another client who gets up at 4 am Monday through Friday to work out because her physical and mental health are non-negotiable to her. What are you willing to sacrifice to make your dreams a reality?

Your Type Matters

All this action is pointless if you don't take action in the right direction, based on who you are. The first three sections of this book are all about a specific roadmap for your type.

Extroverts and Introverts are going to have a different roadmap and different directions in their business. They have different sources of energy, and therefore need to set up their days differently. One of my clients is part of an extremely successful direct selling company that is co-owned by two powerful females. They share the CEO responsibilities of the company. One is an ISTJ and the others is an ENFP. The ISTJ is perfectly comfortable being behind the scenes; in fact, she prefers it. The ENFP is the face of the company; she does all the speaking on stage, videos, and most of the training. They make it work knowing their innate preferences for Introversion and Extroversion.

Sensors and Intuitives are very different. Sensors have a preference for daily routines, details, facts, and are perfectly fine with the 9-5. Intuitives, on the others hand, "suck" at those things and must design a different life for themselves, specifically a different career, or they are destined to be unhappy and unfilled.

Thinkers and Feelers also need to design a different roadmap based on their preferences for how they make decisions and their level of comfort with decisions based on feeling or logic (thinking).

Lastly, Judgers and Perceivers are going to have to understand their innate differences about how they like to be organized in this world. This understanding is essential for them to be able to have a successful business, as well as some down time to enjoy the other things in life.

Getting Unstuck

I cannot tell you how many people stay stuck because they don't know who they are and they don't design, visualize, and plan a life for themselves. They live a life that others have decided they should live, which is totally crazy.

Like many of you, this is indeed my story. I was told to shush, just go along, get your head out of the clouds, get a "real job," and people won't pay for that. I was asked, "Are you sure that is what you want to do?" I am sure you can think of a few things people have said to you along the way. We must get that garbage out of our heads and put positive things back in so we can create our own lives!

It's great for you to explore your thoughts and beliefs, but until you put your plan into action—until there is momentum behind your thinking—nothing is going to happen. You are just being entitled until you take action! The only way for you to get unstuck and start to Live Your Life from the Front Seat is for you to start doing.

You have to take action. Even the smallest action, done consistently, yields results.

Two of the best books I have ever read about taking action are Jeff Olson's *The Slight Edge* and Gay Hendricks' *The Big Leap*. I have pulled out one concept from each book that I think will help you tremendously until you can read each of them yourself, which I highly recommend.

Gay Hendricks talks about a concept in his book that I like to refer to as *The Big Leap* Ball. Imagine yourself with one of those bouncy exercise balls. You are holding it in your hands. You can also imagine this diagram.

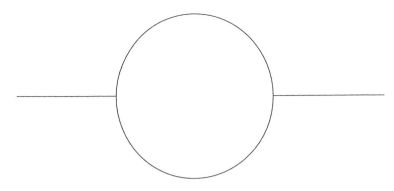

On the *left of the ball* is where you are right now in your business. Get honest for a minute about where that is. Take a moment to write it out. You may still be in a 9-5 job, you may have started your own business and only have a couple of clients, you may be fully in your business and want to start leveraging yourself, or you may be earning $10,000 a month and want to grow to $50,000. You must know where you are starting, so take a moment to make some notes about where you are in your business as of today.

_____

_____

_____

_____

_____

_____

_____

_____

_____

Now on the *right side of the ball* is where you want to go in your life and business. Think back to the third section of this book. What did you dream about? What did you put on your vision board? What is on your goal cards? What are you journaling about? What do you envision when you are meditating? This is exactly what goes on the right of the ball. Take a moment to write out a few of those things you desire in your life and business. This may be a house in Maui, an amazing relationship, joy, $50,000 a month, doing a TedTalk, or publishing a book.

_____

_____

_____

_____

_____

_____

_____

_____

_____

_____

_____

_____

_____

Now, *the ball represents your ego*! Your ego is inside you and designed to keep you safe, but not safe in a good way, safe as in complacent. Your ego tells you false things to keep you from pushing to the next level. It might give you the message that you are not smart enough or creative enough, or that nobody is going to buy your services. Take a moment to write down what your ego tells you because it's important to be aware. When those messages creep in, and they will, you have to be able to recognize them and choose to block and push past them.

My ego is a real bitch; she says horrible things to me and when she creeps up it is my job to push and push and push past her until I pop the ball and get to the other side, which is what I have been visualizing and working toward. It is exhilarating to get to that other side and realize you have pushed through the limiting beliefs of your ego. You did it!

However, there is a little bit of bad news that comes along with this great sense of accomplishment. The ball keeps moving. You will have a new set of fears to overcome as your dream keeps growing. The good news is once you have done it, you know you can do it again and again and again. The sign of a truly successful entrepreneur is to be able to grow, create, adapt, and pivot as needed. Never ever stop growing. Never.

This is where Jeff Olson's idea of the 5% in *The Slight Edge* comes in. Olson says in his book that consistent, small steps, every single day is what yields long-term huge results, not some false quantum leap. It takes consistency and dedication on an ongoing basis to create lasting and sustainable results. I totally agree!

I have taken his concept that approximately 5% of people are actually willing to do what is necessary and applied it to *The Big Leap* ball concept. What most people—Olson would say 95% of them—do is run with the ball until it gets too hard so they give up. Imagine running into a wall with that exercise ball in your hands. You are going to hit that wall hard and bounce back to your place of complacency. Most people will try once, twice, maybe even five times, but then they give up and stay in the place to the left of the ball (in the life they are in now). Olson suggests only about 5% of the population—the 5%ers—actually have what it takes to push past that ego ball to get to the other side. Which one are you?

Are you part of the 95% of the population that gives up and stays complacent, or are you willing to do the daily, consistent, hard work it takes to be a 5%er and push through that ego ball and get to the other side? Let's finish strong and learn how to push through that ball to get you to the other side.

Codependency and Personal Responsibility

Since this chapter is all about taking action, this is a good place to remind you about the power of codependency. Here is a quick reminder of what the tennis court interaction looks like: Instead of playing their tennis game from their own side of the court, they are constantly jumping back and forth over the net—onto their opponent's side and back to their side—trying to manage the whole game.

Codependent people (1) allow others to control them out of doing what they need to do for themselves, or (2) they are too busy managing and controlling other people to look at their own shit. Both stay stuck.

This chapter is truly about personal responsibility. You will never get anywhere in life without taking personal responsibility for your own actions. You choose what you put in your mouth every day to fuel your body. You choose to get up early to do your journaling and meditation. You choose to be nice to the person at the grocery store. You choose to stay in an unhealthy relationship and do nothing about it. You choose to stay in that shitty job and not change your attitude, go back to school, or find another one.

You are in charge of your life (along with God/the Universe's help), so you have nobody to blame but yourself if your life isn't the way you want it. Put on your big girl panties and start taking some action toward the life you want to live. Please. I implore you. I don't even know you, but I want this for you. I want it for everyone.

First and foremost, you must accept responsibility for your own actions that are causing you to feel unhappy and unsatisfied with life. You may have some messy circumstances in your life right now; you are not entirely without blame for that mess. It didn't all happen to you; you helped in some way to create the life you are living. You are, in part, responsible for the life you are leading.

Take the time to do the heavy lifting and take responsibility for your thoughts, beliefs, and actions that have brought you to where you are today. This isn't an easy thing to do, and it is easy to get caught up in feeling that you should just give up.

Stop beating yourself up. You have dreams and lofty amazing goals. You can achieve them. All of them.

Yes, you can do this, but most of us need help; it is OK to ask for help. I got help. I still get help. You don't have to do this alone; it is much easier and actually more fun to create an amazing life with someone loving by your side. You cannot allow someone else's unhappiness with themselves affect the work you are meant to do in this world.

Please stop being a victim or a martyr and start taking personal responsibility for your own life, your own happiness, and your own success or failures. You can do this; it is on you. Are you ready to learn about the Three S's that are guaranteed to help you in your business (if you do them and take action)?

The Three S Method™

As a result of working for years with countless clients, I have come up with a coaching process I call The Three S Method™, which stands for structure, systems, and singular focus. Making these three techniques a priority will change your business and your life forever. I guarantee it.

So many people try to put the cart before the horse and then can't figure out why their business isn't working. You Ps are not going to like this, but you need to pay attention. I recently had a conversation with a client who admitted she'd been resisting this idea of giving structure to her life. She pushed back against me, but finally after almost a year of wasted time she realized that this simple step is what has been holding back her success. She is a P and likes to stay up late, get up late, and take things day by day. She likes to choose her actions for the day based on how she is feeling. Her approach to life doesn't work! It might work for a teenager, but not for adults with a vision of a magnificent life and successful business.

Let me tell you about the CEO mentality. If you're an adult operating a business, it's time for you to develop this mentality. CEOs work their asses off, especially CEOs of their own companies. Ask yourself right now—this very moment—how you spend your time. Get out your journal and write down how you spend your time. Be honest.

- When do you wake up in the morning?
- When do you go to bed at night?
- How do you spend your time each morning?
- How much time do you spend on Facebook, Instagram, or Pinterest?
- When do you do your laundry?
- What are your TV watching habits?
- How often during the week do you go to lunch with friends?
- How much time do you spend actually doing your job—billable hours?
- How much time do you spend working on your business to improve processes, develop sellable products and services, and expand your visibility?

I read in a book about a coach who asked his client (a writer), "How do you spend your day?" She went on to describe her day outlining the following choices:

- Out of bed *around* 7:00 a.m.
- Made the kids' lunches
- Woke up her kids, fed them breakfast, and got them off to school

- Checked Facebook
- Ate breakfast
- Did some laundry
- Went grocery shopping
- Attended a yoga class
- Ate lunch
- Showered
- Sat down to do some writing before picking up her kids from school at 2:45 p.m.

The coach said, "Great. So you are a stay-at-home mom with a possible hobby of writing." The woman was angry and offended, but the coach simply interpreted how she spends her time.

You need to take inventory of how you are spending your time and determine the correlation with your business success. As an entrepreneur you may work from home, but if you went to an office, your kids wouldn't come knocking on your door asking for a snack. If you want your business to succeed you have to start treating it as a priority, giving it priority time and energy.

Structure

I am sure you can see where I am going here: you need some structure! No, a structured day isn't always fun or spontaneous, but I choose a kick-ass company, a great income, leaving a legacy, and changing people's lives over sleeping in. That's just me. What about you? What do you choose?

You likely haven't made it this far in the book if the latter is true. So stop acting like a spoiled, entitled teenager and get your shit together. It's a choice I promise you will not regret.

Recently I had a new client tell me she *couldn't* get up earlier. I paused and said, "You can; it is a choice." She finally came to realize how silly and limiting her thinking was. It was awesome to watch her come to this conclusion right before my eyes.

It's so easy to get caught up in your old limiting ways of being that you may forget that everything is a choice. I am not the only one who suggests structuring your day. Basically, every successful person ever in the history of the world does the things I am suggesting. In this section about structure we are going to discuss the following tools: a daily schedule, morning practice, journaling, books, and meditation.

Daily Schedule

The first step of structure is to give yourself a specific time Monday through Friday to go to bed at night and rise each morning. Unless you are a DJ or own a night club, you should be in bed between 9-11 pm. I also suggest getting up at or before 6 am. That's it. Simple.

Morning Practice

Hal Elrod wrote a great book called, *The Morning Miracle: The Not-So-Obvious Secret Guaranteed to Transform Your Life (Before 8 AM)*. It's an awesome resource if you need more than I am about to share with you.

Five days a week I get out of bed at 5:30 am and spend 30-90 minutes doing what I call my morning practice. I even do this every day except Sunday, when I allow myself to sleep in. I even do this practice while on vacation.

Before you roll your eyes because you may have heard about this before, let me give you a few more reasons following a morning practice will change your life:

> **You will start your day being *proactive* instead of *reactive*.** Think about those days when you get up late and rush around the house to shower and get the kids ready to go.

You're barely making it out the door on time and you didn't have time to make yourself a healthy lunch. You're in a reactive stance because you *chose* not to give yourself enough time to have a proactive morning. When I am proactive, I make a choice to get up way earlier than I need to. I may not technically start seeing clients until 9 am, but I certainly don't sleep in until 8 am. No way.

I know plenty of people who get up early so they can start each day calmly. I promise you that having a morning practice of calm activities (i.e., journaling, exercising, stretching, meditating, visualizing, sitting alone, being quiet) will change you on the inside. It is as important to me each day as brushing my teeth. I still see so many people being reactive to everything around them. Observing them stresses me out. It's no way to live. It is simply a choice.

You will feel grounded. The second huge benefit to a morning practice is that it grounds you, meaning you feel attached to, and in balance with, the Earth. The world is going to push you around and demand things of you. If you aren't grounded, you'll be knocked down and feel off kilter. I think of morning practice as a way for you to cement yourself to the ground. It's a way to connect to your thoughts, beliefs, and emotions. If you don't know those things about yourself, you are bound to follow others foolishly or get sucked into the codependency trap. When you're grounded, you have a much stronger voice and opinion because you're aware of what you think, believe, and feel. It never ceases to amaze me how many people have *no* idea what they want in life or how they feel about something. It's because they don't take the time to figure it out. You will *never* get to where you want to go in your life and business until you take the time daily to figure out what you think, feel, and believe, and how to express those things through your choices and actions.

You become your priority. I realize many of you may think making yourself your priority is selfish, and I really need you to just get over that. It is old school thinking that needs to go away. You cannot be your best for your business, your employees, your clients, and your family if you are not first and foremost always taking care of yourself. Ok, are we done with this? We have so much else to learn. Make yourself your priority and everything else will fall in line after that, I promise.

Your ideas will come to you. Imagine for a moment being in that chaotic energy when you are frantic and busy. That chaotic energy acts as a force field against ideas, and as entrepreneurs, ideas are your life. You *must* get quiet in order for your ideas to make themselves known and for you to give your ideas the consideration they deserve. When do your best ideas come to you? Are you walking in nature, enjoying some down time, journaling, or meditating? For some of you, your best ideas may come when you're having a lovely and calm conversation with a friend or colleague. Ninety-nine percent of my ideas come to me during my morning practice. That's why it's a priceless choice I make every day.

I start my morning practice with coffee, always. Then, I do each of the following activities, but in no particular order.

Gratitude Journal

Journaling is meant to transfer your ideas and thoughts from your head onto paper. I call the process of journaling *externalizing the crazy* because running your own business can certainly make you feel crazy at times. I have many journals going at one time—one for my free-writing, another for "aha" business ideas, and the last is for my daily gratitude. I start every morning sitting in my big comfy chair, writing in all three. Next to me is my favorite table, which holds my books, journals, fresh flowers, and a lit candle.

A daily gratitude journal can dramatically change your attitude toward your life, yourself, and others. Choosing to see the positive aspects of each day is a conscious decision, and one I choose to make daily. I suggest you do the same.

When I first started doing this practice I assumed each day I'd write about the same things: my family, my health, blah, blah, blah. Much to my surprise, I had unique things on my list every single day. There is so much to be grateful for when we take the time to pay attention and write down the positive aspects of our choices and actions.

Being grateful about our life partners is powerful. If you find yourself nitpicking everything your partner does wrong, start a gratitude journal for all the things s/he does right and the things you love. The list will start to grow. Also, start making a conscious effort to do nice things for them—it could change your relationship.

The same applies for your business, money, and employees. Whatever we choose to focus on grows. Deal with the problems head on, but choose to focus on the good, which will grow, I promise. For example, if I am thankful that I have enough money to pay a bill that day, even if I don't want to pay it, showing gratitude for having the money will allow it to grow. Remember that positivity begets positivity. Negativity begets negativity. Choose positivity every day.

Each morning, I simply start writing on a new page with the date. I start by writing: Today I am grateful for... Sometimes the list is longer than others, but there is always something on the list.

Books

Books and reading are great ways to explore new ideas and to shift your mindset. However, not everyone enjoys sitting down and reading a book. For some, it's too boring to read. For others, they aren't getting enough pretty pictures. Others find it hard to focus on the page and would prefer to listen to a lecture or an audio book. Everyone learns differently, and all those ways are perfectly okay.

While I believe reading novels is an excellent practice for entrepreneurs, we *need* to be reading excellent business books! My group coaching clients receive a new book to read every quarter. We read the books together as a group and discuss the content and the insights that result.

Daily reading of books as part of your morning practice is a constant source of new information for your mind, body, and soul. I never wake up and turn on the news. Ever. I do not want to start my day with the negativity of what is going on in our world. Remember, what we think about all day we become. The news is good for what it is, but it is also filled with fear and worry and I do not want that in my soul. I choose to start my day calmly exploring ideas through activities and books that feed my soul.

Here are some of the books I may choose to read during my morning practice:

- *The Language of Letting Go* by Melody Beattie
- *Jesus Calling* by Sarah Young
- *Sacred Rebels Oracle: Guidance for Living a Unique and Authentic Life* by Alana Fairchild and Autumn Skye Morrison

- *Goddess Guidance Oracle Cards* by Doreen Virtue
- Any book written by Alan Cohen
- My personal goal cards

Meditation

Meditation is a practice of getting quiet and bringing your attention back to your breath, which is the center of all life. We are all bombarded with outside stimuli these days and can lose our primary focus, which should always be on ourselves and the purpose of our lives.

There's an epidemic going on in the world right now: people are way too busy and don't know how to just be. As a super J, I had to learn how to shut down all the expectations of myself and simply *be*. For me and all the Js out there, meditating may take some work, but it is necessary for mental and physical well-being, the health of our relationships, and the success of our businesses. We cannot always be on the go.

There is a saying that if we don't take time to slow down, our bodies will do it for us by creating an illness that will shut us down. I have certainly experienced that, haven't you? I actually schedule fake sick days into my life. On those days, I do what I would do if I were sick: sleep in, turn off my phone, take naps, watch TV all day, and eat whatever I want. These are scheduled days of rest. I am also an A+ vacationer; I work hard and I play hard. I suggest you start implementing some down time into your life. A great way to start is by meditating every day.

I have a number of clients who, when they start working with me, don't know how to just *be*. They always need to have the TV on, be talking on the phone, managing someone, or working. They are constantly doing, doing, doing. There is typically a lot of self-imposed chaos in their lives. You know these people, right? You might even be one of them. Let me fill you in on a little secret, you aren't very fun to be around.

For all the people who can't get off their phone because they forgot what it is like to actually sit and connect themselves with another live human being, this section of the book may challenge you. But if you don't take time to slow down, clear your mind, get centered, and figure out who the heck you are and what you want in life, you are *never* going to get it. You will keep living a reactionary life. I want you to live a proactive life. Do you know you can have that? Yes, you can, but *you* have to create it.

When people hear the word meditation, many images come to mind. Often there is the image of the Master seated in a lotus pose with the incense swirling to the breeze in a still, quiet garden. They imagine having to sit still for a long time, being quiet, emptying their mind and chanting mantras in a foreign language. Unfortunately, many Western people (Americans and Europeans) still think of meditation in this way. In fact, I used to hate the word meditation.

As a strong Extrovert, the idea of sitting and meditating held absolutely no appeal to me. I have learned that there are as many ways to meditate as there are types of people. Meditation is not one thing for everybody. Meditation for one person might be taking a walk, for another it might be going through a garden, for another it might be sitting outside. You don't have to close your eyes to meditate; you can meditate with your eyes open. You can do guided meditations or unguided meditations. But when it comes down to it, meditation is taking the time to be alone, get quiet, clear your mind, and breathe. It is a reflective (looking inward) exercise that can bring a lot of clarity to problems or simply bring insight.

We all need down time. We can choose to numb out and binge watch Netflix (which has its time and place), but better yet, we can choose to be mindful of our down time and simply meditate. The definition of mindfulness is to pay attention on purpose, so pay attention to your down time and truly enjoy it.

It still amazes me how many people find this practice of selecting time that is just for you as being selfish. I truly believe it is selfish not to honor yourself with personal time. We simply cannot be our best selves if we are not grounded in who we are. This entire book is about exactly that, and the practice of meditation is the best of all these techniques. Think of it as time to get reconnected to your core, your breath, and yourself.

Meditation is like a muscle; the more you work out, the stronger you will become. When you are just getting started, your mind will wander often. Don't judge it; just notice and bring yourself back by paying attention to your breathing. You will get better. When I first started meditating, I spent a lot of time judging myself for doing it wrong. Then I realized, as I do with most things, "I am doing it, which is what is most important. There is no perfect way." The Dalai Lama has even said he still has a wandering mind when meditating. Don't judge yourself; just do it.

Most Extroverts prefer guided visual meditations, especially to start. There are literally thousands on iTunes, but I have provided a few of my favorites at the back of this book. I still use these and love them.

You can meditate anywhere you like. I like to meditate in my imaginary treehouse. You might prefer to meditate in a park. your own house, or by the beach. The important thing is simply for you to feel safe and comfortable so you can enter into a relaxed, meditative state.

The next thing to consider is the best time for you to meditate. If you're a morning person, waking up a bit earlier to take that time to meditate could help you start the day off well. If you're a night owl, maybe meditating when everyone else has gone to bed will give you the opportunity to go deep into yourself to get new perspectives and insight. It's tough to meditate when the kids are pulling on you and demanding attention, or when your boss is yelling for you to hand over that report, or when your partner needs your help with something. Choose your best time and commit to taking that time every day, no matter what, even if it is just a few minutes.

I like to spend my few minutes in between clients closing my eyes or looking at the water outside my office and getting myself centered back to my breath. It is the best way to get myself centered so I can then give my best to my next client. Think about how you could incorporate that into your life with your children, spouse, and clients.

Different meditations lend themselves to different ways and times to do them. One of my friends uses super-short hypnosis meditations (seven minutes long) twice a day— morning and night—to help her get stay focused and feel more positive about her circumstances. Another person I know says that she's joined the 5 am Club. This mother and entrepreneur wakes every day at 5 o'clock in the morning so that she can meditate, exercise, and focus on her goals.

No matter what style of meditation you choose, simply taking the time to do this every day can help you take leaps and bounds in the right direction for your life.

Your Structure

This section is meant to give you some action steps for the roadmap you created earlier so I encourage you to review your personal structure. Which of the tools I've suggested are part of your daily routine? What might you add to keep your business on track? Which actions might you choose to start implementing?

I encourage you to make some notes before we move on to *Systems* and *Single Focus*. We are going to cover a lot of information in the coming pages and if you don't have a plan and a personal structure, implementing the systems and staying focused aren't going to happen. You will stay stuck. And stuck sucks.

Systems

Now that you have a structure to follow, we must talk about the systems necessary to create a thriving business and successful life. This may seem overwhelming to some of you, but I never promised all of this would be easy. Remember that you are a 5%er. Ninety-five percent of the population is simply surviving. You want to thrive, so you must create and implement systems that support you to know where you're going and take action to get there. Everything we've talked about so far is pointless if you don't take what you've learned and add consistent action to your dreams and plans.

Let's talk about systems to keep your business in A+ shape. The systems we are going to discuss in this section are a weekly plan, core values, masterminding, accountability, coaching, and 90-day focus.

Your Weekly Plan

You already know a morning practice is important for starting your day well. In order for your week to be productive, having a weekly schedule is critical for every entrepreneur. Part of the reason many of us started working for ourselves was to make and follow our own schedule, but this is where we often fall into a trap and lose the freedom we desire. The key to maintaining freedom is having a schedule and following the plan. Without a schedule, unproductive activities seep into our week and before we know it we aren't working at all; we're completely unproductive.

> **Schedule your week.** You must set a schedule for yourself each week. Every day might look a bit different, which is excellent for Intuitives. We love the variety each week brings. But there must be days you work *in* your business and days you work *on* your business.

Working *in* your business means that you are actually doing the work, such as serving your clients, writing, marketing, and selling a product. Then there must be as least a half day each week that you work *on* your business, which I call your CEO meeting. This is time where you send invoices, review your balance sheet, plan, update your calendar, and set up meetings. I encourage you to take time right now to write down your CEO meeting tasks. What are the tasks in your business that only you can do? These are critically important to the long-term success of your business.

If you don't take this time each week you are living five minutes in front of your face and you are likely going to fail. Successful entrepreneurs spend time each week working *on* and *in* their business. What is the best day and time for you to work *on* your business? I suggest scheduling time each Friday so you can assess how the week went and how you can improve in the coming week. Be proactive and plan your next week on Friday.

Stop having business lunches. Realistically, business lunches take three hours out of your day. If people want to meet with you to connect one-on-one to network, great. Make them come to you for a 30-minute chat or use Facetime, Zoom, or Skype. One of the suggestions I have for my clients is to set up shop one day a week in a coffee shop and have people come to you throughout the day. Or, if you have an office, invite them to meet you there. From this point forward, you are not allowed to spend time traveling to one-on-one "get acquainted" meetings. Use technology. I use Zoom and love it. You can still have coffee dates with people, just do so in the comfort of your own workspace or office.

Work from a weekly priority list. Know what is most important to your business. Each week, make a list of the most important tasks to accomplish and make them a priority. I suggest doing those tasks first thing in the morning (after your morning practice, of course). When you look at your calendar, the priority tasks need to make up the majority of your calendar time.

Use a calendar. Don't get fancy; simply use the calendar on your phone. Or use a paper calendar. (I know business owners who still do.) I use the Outlook calendar religiously. Everything about my business life is on there. Everything!

Using a calendar is easier for Js than Ps, but we both need to use the tool. Ps can also benefit greatly from a yearly and weekly visual calendar. Ps innately live five minutes in front of their faces, but they all want to be more planned. I have an erasable weekly calendar on my fridge and find it extremely helpful for work and personal planning. For all you Ps, during your next CEO meeting, put all your tasks and activities into your electronic calendar. You may also want to take a picture so you can reference it during the week, or save it as your screen background for the week.

Annually, I buy a wall calendar as soon as they come out in June so I can start planning the coming year. If you are in a place in your business where you can hire a part-time or full-time assistant, you must hire someone with a J Type. Have them take my assessment and allow them to lead you, plan for you, and keep you on track. A colleague of mine hired an assistant for 20 hours a month specifically to manage her. It's changed her business life dramatically. Important stuff meant to attract new clients is getting done, finally. It will elevate your business and keep your mind clear to do the things you are supposed to be doing.

Core Values

My second favorite tool to help you learn who you are is a core values exercise. Of course, knowing your personality Type is my number one favorite.

While Type is innate and does not change, core values are learned and can change throughout your life. Therefore, the tools are a great pairing to help guide you in every decision you make. Obviously, I design my life around my personality Type as I want all of you to do as well. My core values are a gauge for deciding who and what I allow into my life. I bounce every business opportunity that comes into my life off my core values to make sure it is a fit. My core values are:

- **Freedom**—Does this person or opportunity allow me to have the freedom I desire in my life?
- **Authenticity**—Does this person or opportunity allow me to fully be me without judgment?
- **Love**—Does this person or opportunity allow me to give and receive love?
- **Inspiration/Inspire**—Does this person or opportunity inspire me and allow me a chance to inspire?
- **Powerful**—Does this person or opportunity allow me to fully be in my personal power without intimidating them?

What are your core values? How do they factor into your life? Do some things need to be cut out because they aren't in alignment with your current values?

When I first identified my core values I discovered how much my 15-year marriage did not allow me to experience my values. It was a huge eye-opening insight. I had to figure out who I was. I married someone and we had built a relationship where my core values did not have a place to exist. My realization was painful and validating. Once our marriage was over I decided to never allow someone or something into my life where I wasn't fully able to be my full ENFJ self and able to live in alignment with my core values of freedom, authenticity, love, inspiration, and power.

I encourage you to do the core values exercise with as little judgment as possible. The values reveal important information about how you feel. You have to figure out who you are if you want to finally be happy and successful. Quit giving yourself up to other people and things. I did it for many, many years and I pray for nothing more than for you to avoid those same mistakes. Happiness truly comes from knowing who you are and designing life accordingly.

Please go to my website **www.jessicabutts.com** now and print out the core values exercise and the instructions on what to do. This is an amazing exercise to do with business and life partners. Along with personality type, these two exercises will give you more information into who they are and how best to treat them. I love having a roadmap to give others on how to love, respect, and treat me—and I equally love having one for them as well. Have fun!

Masterminding

Since one of the best things you can add into your life is like-minded people, this next system is important.

Masterminds are small groups of four to six people, typically other entrepreneurs, whom you trust to give you ideas on your business. You want people who have a fresh perspective and can generate ideas you wouldn't think of. Being an entrepreneur or solopreneur can be lonely and isolating, especially in this world of so many Sensing Types that may not support our dreams. It is imperative to have this group of trusted people in your life to meet with regularly, optimally monthly or quarterly, for extended periods of time.

I meet quarterly for a weekend with my mastermind group. We work on our mind maps and plan the next 90 days. Then we hold each other accountable on a weekly basis until the next time we meet. We have a private Facebook page where we can connect between meetings to vent or ask questions. Each of us also has an accountability partner we meet with weekly or bi-weekly.

While you can certainly spend some time socializing in the beginning, this is not a social group and needs to be treated as seriously as you treat your business. So set an agenda, be on time, stick to it, be helpful, come prepared, and do what you say you are going to do. My mastermind is my trusted group of advisors and I value our time together more than I can say.

Accountability Partners

As I mentioned above, an accountability partner is the person you check in with on a regular basis to help each other stay on track with your business goals. I like to think of time with an accountability partner as Weight Watchers for your business. For those of you who have been part of Weight Watchers, you know what it feels like to look ahead to your public weigh-in. It really helps keep you on track with your eating and most importantly, it helps keep it top of mind all the time. Your accountability partner check-in calls should function similarly; they're meant to help you keep your priorities top of mind.

You need to weigh in daily or weekly with your accountability partner so you think about how you are spending your time and if you are doing what you said you were going to do. If not, why? That is a question only you can answer and it is a *very* important question we all need to ask ourselves often. Why aren't I doing what I said I was going to do? Am I not interested in the work? Am I making excuses? Am I eating food that fuels my body? Am I trying to work at times during the day that are not productive for me? Am I trying to do too many things at once? Am I getting distracted by Facebook, laundry, TV, or email? There are a million reasons why we can lose motivation so we *must* ask ourselves why.

While writing this book I had days full of distractions. It is a long and difficult process writing a quality book. I would call my book coach Karen and we would discuss why. For me, giving myself too much time, like an entire day or a weekend away, does not work. My best time for writing is first thing each morning for about two hours. I liked to get the work out of the way so I could go about my day. What works for you will likely be different, but you must ask yourself why. Get curious with yourself and your accountability partner.

This is structured time, not social time. Divide the time evenly between the two of you. Be prepared to share about your progress and to be helpful to your partner. Listen, get curious, challenge them, help them, and provide suggestions. Most importantly, do not tell them what to do. This person will become your trusted confidant, but it takes time to grow into that relationship. Have some patience because having this person in your life can and will change your business.

Coaching

Get a coach! Everyone needs a coach; I have a coach. Need I say more?

Ok, I will say a little more.

Choose someone you respect and want to be like and who has a business model you want. Hiring a coach is an investment that plants a stake in the ground declaring you are serious about building a business. It is not a hobby. Every person I know, every single person, who thinks they can do it on their own either fails or it takes them 10 times longer to accomplish their goals. You cannot and should not build a business alone. I don't know about you, but I don't have 10 times longer. When I first started, I was impatient and wanted successful results immediately. I had a vision, but I didn't know how to get there, so I hired someone who had already done it. People, we don't need to reinvent the wheel. Hire someone awesome who has already done what you want to do and then put your own spin on it! I guess I did need to say more. Get a coach!

90-Day Plan

Once you have a mind map you are ready to take that information and put it into action. I am obsessed with 90-day focus sheets. My first coach, Fabienne Fredrickson, introduced me to these 90-day sheets and I have been consistently using them for many years. Nothing, I mean nothing, helps you stay on track more than 90-day focus sheets. Here is a diagram of what one looks like, but I have also added the sheet to my resources page on my website under The Book tab at www.jessicabutts.com so you can print them and use them at your leisure.

List the *most* important three items from your mind map on this 90-day focus sheet. *Most* important should be the things that need to happen *now* to help you get all the rest of those wonderful dreams on that mind map done. Building a business and growing it takes steps. You cannot jump from where you are now to the end; you must do things in order and step-by-step. Again, a good coach, mastermind group, or my workbook for this book will help you know which steps to do at the appropriate time. You *must* build the foundation *first*.

The 90-day focus sheets are designed to help you stay on track with the things that are highest priority so you can build a successful long-term business. The overarching idea is that you are *only* allowed to focus on three things for the next 90 days. The bright shiny objects that show up are not allowed to come in and distract you from those three things. This is critically important, especially for Intuitives, because you like bright and shiny objects, but they are your downfall. You must stay focused in order to be successful.

I have been coaching for years and the number one problem I see with entrepreneurs is they do not set up successful structures and systems and they fail to stick to a singular focus. All the dreaming in the world is not going to get you anything without

Specific Goal	Ideal Outcome	Obstacles	Strategies to Overcome Obstacle	First Step
1. Target Date:				
2. Target Date:				
3. Target Date:				

focus! Please, please, please pay attention to The Three S Method™. Nobody can hear your message if you don't get your shit together. You must take those ideas and consistently put structure to them. Weekly CEO meetings, weekly accountability calls, quarterly mastermind groups, a great coach, and actually doing what you say you are going to do are key to your success. You can do this, even you Ps!

I have coached hundreds of Ps into successful structures, systems, and singular focus. Most of them are now are world-changers because they chose to learn how to do what I am teaching you. If you want more of this, check out the digital workbook for this book called *Roadmap to YOUR Front Seat Life.* I add videos and extra tools to help you implement The Three S Method™ because I know how important this is to your success. Are you ready to quit making excuses and do something about it? Good. Let's move on to the final S, which is singular focus.

Singular Focus

Now that we have covered the critical importance of structure in your life and systems to make you successful, it is time to discuss the last S, singular focus. Most entrepreneurs are entrepreneurs for a reason: they have an abundance of ideas and they love to think outside the box. This is a blessing and a curse. Great ideas are a blessing, but it becomes a curse when you can't stay focused on one idea.

Here's the deal. You must concentrate on and develop one idea before moving on to the next one. Flitting from one thing to another is not part of the recipe for success. You are allowed to take one singular focus and scale it like crazy. However, you are not allowed to shift your attention from one thing to the next. Why?

- Singular focus gives you traction to being recognized as the expert in the field.
- You get known for that idea and your colleagues know how to refer to you.

- You establish a solid reputation as a credible and confident business person.
- People learn to trust you because they know what you stand for.

In this section about having singular focus, we are going to discuss the *know, like, and trust factor; zone of genius; your energy; compartmentalization; your mess is your message; point of view; niche; and like-minded people.*

Know, Like, Trust

The *know, like, trust factor* is a well-known concept in networking. You must get out there and *get known* for a specific idea. Connecting with your target market in person and by sharing content via social media and email is required.

Vanilla, bland, boring people are easily forgotten. People who stand out and take a stand for something—have a singular focus, almost an obsession—are hard to forget. Get known for something, just one thing, and stick to it.

The next step is to be *liked*. As you may recall I take a hard stance on this because not everyone is going to like you. Get over it. The key to being liked comes down to doing things authentically to who you are (your personality Type). Don't fake it trying to be like everyone else. Be *you*. You now know who you are so there are no excuses. Do your thing, do it hard, do it consistently, and your ideal clients will show up and stay.

Lastly, there is *trust*. The definition of trust is the firm belief in the reliability, truth, ability, or strength of someone or something. So be consistent in your messaging and stop flitting from one thing to the other. Be someone people can trust. Otherwise they are never going to do business with you. Period.

Zone of Genius

An excellent exercise to help you figure out what you are great at and the things you suck at (and need to delegate) is the Zone of Genius map I have lovingly borrowed from Gay Hendricks' work in *The Big Leap*.

We all have things we are innately good at and things we suck at doing. God designed us this way so quit trying to fight it.

The Zone of Genius is yet another tool to help you gain deeper clarity on what you need to be spending your time doing and what you must learn to delegate as a business owner.

Let's walk through the zone quadrants, beginning with the bottom two.

Zone of Genius	Zone of Excellence
Zone of Competence	Zone of Incompetence (AKA, Stuff You Suck At)

The Zone of Incompetence is basically all the stuff that is your Drunk Uncle (all the things you suck at). You should already have a list of what those things are. One of the best things you can do for your business today is to immediately hire an assistant and delegate those activities. Stop doing them! Remember, it is like a drunk person trying to do them, so stop wasting your precious energy on them.

The Zone of Competence is where the majority of people spend most of their time being competent. I refer to this zone as complacency. You are fine at doing these things. In fact, you can do them in your sleep; you're very competent. Sadly, this is what most people settle for in their lives. Ugh! That is the worst thing I can think of: living a *fine* life. God put you on this earth for a very short period of time, and it is your responsibility to do the most with your innate gifts and talents, so please quit wasting your time on *fine*.

Make a list of all the of things in your business that take up your energy and someone else could do for you. If you are just starting out, you will need to start with an assistant who can do the Zone of Incompetence tasks first.

Where you need to be spending your precious time and energy is in the two top zones, which is where the magic happens and where you really start to make some money.

The Zone of Excellence rules! Have you been there? When you're in this zone you feel on fire. This is where you make good money. The tasks are easy for you; you're in your Front Seat with your Driver and Copilot working together. This is a great place to spend a good amount of time in your business. You are happy here.

However, there is one last quadrant and this quadrant, in my opinion, is much smaller than the rest: it is your Zone of Genius. Not many people get to a place where they get to experience their Zone of Genius because not that many people push past their Zone of Competence. They let fear, rejection, and complacency rule their actions and decisions. You discover this magical place once you have put Living Your Life from the Front Seat and being your authentic personality type into practice for a while.

To enter this zone, you must understand (1) who you are (your Type), (2) where you are going (your mindset and road map), and (3) how you are going to get there (your actions). Once you experience the Zone of Genius, you will never want to go back. You can get there, but it doesn't come without hard work and Living Life from the Front Seat. Do the things I am asking you to do in this book and you'll get there.

Your Energy

When you are thinking about your singular focus, it is imperative to get honest with yourself about where you are spending your time and energy. This cylinder represents 100% of your energy. How much of your precious energy are you spending as your Drunk Uncle doing stuff you suck at? Even worse, how much time and energy are you spending as your Baby in the Back Seat? What percentage would you give to each…35%, 50? More?

How much of your precious energy do you spend:

- worrying about things you cannot do anything about?
- in a bad relationship?
- trying to fix an employee that you should let go?
- feeling tired because you aren't doing things to take care of your body?
- gossiping or talking ill of someone else?
- thinking about incomplete projects?

Get honest about where you are spending your energy because here is a fact: when that cylinder is full, nothing new can come in— no new ideas, no new clients, no new money—until we are willing to flush something out. So take an honest assessment of your energy and what are you willing to get rid of for something new, amazing, and possibly business-changing to come into your life.

Compartmentalization

There is a book called *Men Are Like Waffles, Women are Like Spaghetti: Understanding and Delighting in Your Differences* by Bill and Pam Farrel. To be completely honest, the book is mediocre, but the title is brilliant and so true. The authors use the analogy of pouring syrup. Men's brains are like waffles; the syrup stays in the waffle compartments. Men can separate all aspects of life (i.e. work, kids, marriage, finances, emotions). On the other hand, women's brains are like spaghetti; the syrup runs all over the place and touches everything. There is no compartmentalization.

I have had to teach myself to become more like a man in this area and learn how to compartmentalize things in my life and business. As an entrepreneur your work is never, ever complete. Your business can run into every minute of your life if you let it. Learning to compartmentalize has allowed me to learn how to be 100% present with each person, event, or situation at a time. When I am writing, I am doing it with 100% of my energy. When I am with my family, I am with them 100%. When I am on vacation, I am 100% in chill mode. The alternative is doing 10 different things at 10%. I certainly don't want to give my clients, family, friends, or partner only 10% of my energy and presence. I want them to all have 100% of me when I am with them.

I urge you to practice compartmentalization and you can start by setting a daily schedule for yourself. Get off your phone 24/7, set an end time to your day, and set scheduled times to check your email and social media. You and your loved ones will thank me. Practice being present.

Your Mess is Your Message

One of the best and most true messages I have learned throughout the years of coaching is the popular saying, *your mess is your message*. I am not sure who first said it, but it has come to be popular foundation for successful businesses. It allows you to use your authentic experiences in life to connect to your potential clients, not in a yucky way, but in a true, heart-centered way. When people know you can relate to them by truly understanding their pain, they can connect and trust you. In any business, including and especially small entrepreneurial businesses, you must solve a problem that is causing pain. Your target clients are experiencing similar pain to what you have been through in your life so you can help them solve that problem.

When I was going through the mess of my marriage breaking up, I couldn't help but think my personal experience in this area would be a great asset to help others really understand the specific pain associated with infidelity and addiction. When I started my private therapy practice I knew my mess would be my way to help others, so I started with that niche. I decided to be a therapist to help individuals and couples navigate affairs and/or addictions. I became known for this expertise, and since I did good work, I filled my practice very quickly. People knew how to find me and refer me.

What is your niche? It is likely your mess. A couple good books to help you find your niche are *Purple Cow: Transform Your Business by Being Remarkable* by Seth Godin, and *Start With Why: How Great Leaders Inspire Everyone To Take Action* by Simon Sinek.

You can't just sell shoes, or be a coach, or a designer. You must have a niche so people can find you. When first introduced to this idea people often think, "But aren't I limiting my potential clients?" The answer is yes, and that is OK. You must let our freak flag fly so people know how to find you. Some questions to ask yourself:

- What is your mess?
- What do you believe in?
- What do you stand for?
- How do you specifically work with people?
- Who is your ideal client?
- How do you work with them?
- What tools do you use?
- How do you solve their problem?
- In what sequence do you deliver this?

My first business coach called this a proprietary system. What makes you unique and special? A big part of this relates back to your personality Type. As an Intuitive Type, which many of you reading this are, you are only 25% of the population and therefore see the world very differently than 75% of the world. You see patterns in business, life or relationships that Sensing Types simply don't see. Your mess and your why need to be part of your niche and point of view.

Point of View

My amazing book coach, Karen Lynn Maher, with LegacyOne Authors, teaches about the importance of your *point of view*. If you are going to have a successful business, you must have a *specific* and *powerful* point of view. Basically, why do you care and why should others care? Nobody is going to pay attention to you if you are not clear on your messaging, solve a problem, and have a why.

My client Sarah came to me wanting to establish a coaching practice. She was an excellent coach and had everything in place to get going, but something was missing. She shared all the *hows* of what she does as a coach, but very few *whys*. So, of course, I asked her the million-dollar question, "Why are you passionate about self-care?" She paused and stared at me for a long time. Tears started welling up in her eyes and she continued to tell me her powerful why. I was riveted by the story of how her husband had cheated on her, which hurt her deeply of course, but also destroyed her world and ability to function because she lacked the tools to take care of herself.

Most of us have some story of devastation in our lives and I think those stories give us grit and purpose. Sarah's story conveys her why and makes it possible to connect with people on a deep level. She was reluctant to start sharing her story, but as soon as she did, her business started to grow. She attracts clients left and right because her experience makes it possible for her audience to connect and understand her why. She has a strong point of view and she helps clients solve a real problem because she's been through a similar experience and come through it successfully.

What is your point of view? What is your why? Until you know and can be transparent, authentic, and open, you are likely going to spin your wheels just like Sarah did. So do this work for the sake of your business.

Niche

Your niche is your point of view in action.

Keep asking yourself, "Why do you care? And why should others care?" Once you can match those two questions you have your niche.

There is a huge misconception out there that we should serve everyone so we can keep our net wide and broad and make more money. Wrong! The more niche you can be the better. Let me explain this with some examples:

You sell jewelry, but there has to be more to your offering than simply selling jewelry. Why do you sell jewelry? Who is your ideal client (and it can't be people who want to buy jewelry)? I bet you have a story as to why you went into direct selling. Did you want to be your own boss? Did you want to be home with your kids more? Tell us why. Get deep; get real. The people your story resonates with will become your niche clients for having parties and recruits for your team.

You are a coach or therapist. Who is your ideal client? What is the issue you help your clients solve? Who do you like working with? While Myers-Briggs was always part of my toolbelt I became known for doing great couples work and very quickly filled my practice. As I evolved out of therapy and am now an author, speaker, and coach, I am known for using Myers-Briggs in the unique Front Seat Life way. I work primarily with Intuitive entrepreneurs. I have a niche that has served me very well.

You are a fitness or nutrition educator. There are a million others of you. What is your specific point of view and why? Who do you like working with and why? What is their problem and how do you solve it? I had a client, Taryn, who was a powerhouse fitness and nutrition coach and has four kids. Her specific point of view was to "keep it simple." She liked working with other busy moms. Their problems were her problems as a busy mother who also wanted to keep her health, fitness, and nutrition top of mind. She helps busy moms create simple and easy-to-follow hair, skin, fitness, and nutrition tips and plans. She is brilliant and has created a large following by being completely transparent with her own crazy life and helping others solve the same problems she faces every day. She is working on the best approach to monetizing her coaching expertise, which is best accomplished through private or group coaching.

Take time to really ask yourself:

What is your *specific point of view* and why?
Who do you like working with (your *ideal client*) and why?
What is their *problem* and how do you help them solve it?

When you answer these questions and then start expressing your niche clearly and consistently, your business will grow.

Like-Minded People

I cannot stress enough how important it is to surround yourself with like-minded people. It's really hard to overcome your past and move forward into your goals and future when you hang out with the same people who caused or contributed to your complacency. You need to surround yourself with like-minded people so you have the support you need to be unapologetically who you are.

Sonja, one of my brilliant clients, is a strong INFP who grew up in a Sensing, Thinking and Judging home where she wasn't understood and her creativity was not allowed. Not surprisingly, she married an ESTJ man who also didn't appreciate her creative side. They moved to a community where she continued to suppress her innate self. She came to me miserable, sad, and thinking there was something wrong with her. She viewed herself as a fake and felt unappreciated, alone, and invisible.

Once we uncovered her personality Type, she started to see why she had felt alone, judged, and marginalized most of her life. When she started incorporating like-minded people into her life, she realized how powerful having a community that understands, supports, and loves her can be. She is now a successful author, an amazing loving supportive mother to three wonderful kids, wife to a man who loves and appreciates her, and she is fully able to set boundaries and live the life she was always meant to live. She no longer feels alone. She has a community of people with whom she can truly be herself, without apology.

You can also be surrounded with people who think like you do. You don't have to be alone. A community of like-minded people can take many forms, but it will likely include other entrepreneurs and Intuitive people. There are Facebook groups for people who have similar values and interests. There are book clubs, business clubs, writing groups, and energy groups. Choose a community that excites you and makes you feel more alive, appreciated, connected, and whole. Finding your group of like-minded people can help you express your inner self and be totally authentic.

For the rare Types out there, especially Introverts, Intuitives, Feeling men, and Thinking women, this will be especially important because we are a much smaller percentage of the population. You have likely grown up feeling misunderstood or not "gotten" by many people in your life.

If you're stuck with a group of people who just don't get you, who always make you be something you're not (or that you don't want to be), it's tough to feel validated. You might (and probably will in time) end up losing some of these people who have been a part of your life or simply establish a different relationship with them. That's okay. It is much easier to do this, however, when you are surrounded by others who think and feel like you do. Find them first before you make a lot of changes to your existing community.

If right now you don't know of a group of people who have similar beliefs/experiences/goals/values you do, then maybe the problem isn't that there isn't a community for you. Perhaps it is the Universe asking you to be the one to create that group, to be the magnet for others to feel safe to come out and be themselves with you. Yes, it can be frightening to stop hiding because that's what we do when we're scared. But once you start, more and more people will be drawn to you and your work, and you won't be doing it alone anymore. Be the change you are seeking.

Intuitive, think-outside-the-box, thrivers must hang out with like-minded people or you are subject to getting sucked back into the lack and scarcity mentality of the naysaying world. You have a dream, a passion, a life-changing idea, or mission that you are required by God/the Universe to get out there, and you cannot allow anything or anyone to stop you! You simply cannot.

When I started my therapy practice, I knew I needed to find my tribe, so I went looking. I went to countless therapy groups, support groups, grow-your-business groups, get-client groups, and meet-up groups. None of them were my people. They were too worried about details of this, that, and the other. Who cares? I wanted to grow my business, think outside the box, and find similar people. Then I attended an event by eWomenNetwork. Aha! There they were. A group of entrepreneurial women. They were largely Intuitive types, starting their own businesses, interested in collaboration, helping each other as we grew together. Keep looking for your tribe. They are rare, but they are out there.

You need to find your people. That is why I started my Front Seat Squad, a group of entrepreneurial, Intuitive types whom I coach but who also coach each other. We build each other up when our families or friends don't believe in our dream or don't know how to support us. This isn't just a bunch of head-in-the-clouds women. We call each other out on our shit and help each other get shit done. You need to find those people in your life, or you may want to come join us.

You may be overwhelmed right now, but my hope is you're excited that you have a roadmap to help you make decisive and clear action based on your personality type and the goals we set in *Section 3*. I promised you that if you can start implementing a daily practice, as well as structure, systems, and singular focus into your life, achieving all of your goals is possible. But, you must take action. Action is the final step to creating your Front Seat Life. Quit making excuses and just go do it!

As my wonderful teacher in high school Mr. Rod Sivertson said, "Your life is not a dress rehearsal." This is it, people. Stop messing around. You can have the life you've dreamt of. I've shown you how.

Live your life from the Front Seat™

Everything in this book is meant to help you Live Your Life from the Front Seat and stop doing stuff you suck at. All the promises I make are possible when you are in your Front Seat! Remember that your Front Seat is authenticity—your best self.

The first step is to know your type so you can start visualizing and designing your life around your Front Seat, the way God made you. Then take decisive action toward your goals. If you have done some of these techniques before and they did not work for you, it may be because you were not doing it from your Front Seat. Your Back Seat is fear and doubt; it is yucky, wonky energy. You cannot create the life you desire if you are constantly in the Back Seat.

Remember that small, actionable, and consistent action yields huge results. Here comes some tough love: you cannot do these things for a couple of weeks and then give up because the result you desire didn't happen right away. You must stick with it.

I hope you have taken notes on the pages of this entire book and if you didn't the first time around, you may want to go back and do so when you read it a second time. I also have a digital study guide on my website **www.jessicabutts.com** for those who enjoy learning from video. I also walk people though this quarterly in a group setting so all learning styles can really capture this life-changing content. I want more than anything for you to be successful in your life and business, and taking action is the only way that is going to happen.

Let's wrap this up and get you on your way to Living Your Life from the Front Seat and stop doing stuff you suck at.

Wow, we have come to the end.

As you have learned throughout this book there is a reason you're stuck. There is also a real path to get unstuck. You're ready to start defining who you are, deciding on where you want to go, and plotting your path to get there. That's what works.

Start now! Slide into the front seat of your own life and feel the freedom that your new vision, being unapologetically who you are, and clarity bring to you.

Feel the calm, blissful ease that comes when you focus on one thing and detach from trying to do a million things that never actually get done (and brings on all kinds of guilt).

Know what you stand for! How do you really think and feel? Take personal responsibility for yourself, trusting you can be your best self in whatever role you play—woman, wife, mother, sister, daughter, business owner, employee… doesn't matter. You'll live in integrity, doing what you're innately supposed to be doing, excited to wake up and start the day, not dreading what is to come.

I invite you to make today YOUR day. The day you declare that you're going to only live life from the front seat.

Jump in, let's go for a ride! I will be the best ride of your life!

ABOUT THE AUTHOR

Jessica is a retired psychotherapist turned life and business coach, author, speaker, and trainer. She is on a global mission to help people start living according to their personality Type, be unapologetically who they are, and live happier, more authentic and richer lives. In her business coaching, keynotes, and corporate trainings she teaches audiences three steps: (1) understand and embrace their innateness using the Myers-Briggs Type Indicator® and the Front Seat Life™ system, (2) up-level their mindset, and (3) take action using the Three S Method™. Jessica is an ENFJ and passionate about many things in her life including deep connections with friends and family, Maui, sunsets, travel, and inspiring others to Live their Lives from the Front Seat.